ANALYZE & INFLUENCE PEOPLE

PEOPLE

2 BOOKS IN 1

Analysis of human behavior through the use of body language and manipulation and principles of ethical influence with secret techniques for: handling in people and influencing on social media

FRIEDRICH LLOYD

ANALYZE PEOPLE

Analysis of human behavior through the use
of body language and manipulation, secret
techniques to read people, recognize lies
and mind control

FRIEDRICH LLOYD

Table of Contents

Introduction

This book will look into the subject of analyzing people. Analyzing people is a different dimension and a hectic process in which the person's mind and character are discussed. What are the successive attributes of the person and how that person is able to shape his statements and modes of socialization in any situation? The process of dealing with the human mind is all about analysis and this book will deeply decipher the constructs of analysis properly.

Human behavior will be properly studied. Human behavior is a complex term, in which the values, norms and social orders are deeply considered for the benefit of human behavior. Human behavior precisely deals with this assertion of how people are able to manifest a strong token of appreciation for others and how does this behavior changes with respect to time. For example, according to Montesquieu (1992), human behavior changes with time and in order to make a proper understanding of human behavior, one has to deeply socialize with the subject. Therefore, human behavior is a complex term that tends to make the aspiration of a human engine complete and with this interesting project, the behavior of the human will be periodically discussed.

The importance of body language is yet another topic that will be needing clarification in this book. Body language refers to the use of words, language slogans, language terminologies and language instructs through which the person is able to resonate a strong mode of conviction to others. In terms of other ways, body language is tantamount to proper resonation in the home atmosphere. Body language will always make the human people understand the concept of uniformity in the making and with the passage of time, the people are able to have a strong mode of communication with other people. Body language can be made easy if the person uses a certain amount of tactics through which the body language is deeply affected. These tools will be discussing in brevity in the following pages and there will be a potent use of clarification for other personalities. Thus, the use of body language will enable the person to make the system go way much better.

Reading and detecting people will also be illustrated in this method. The people will understand the primary concepts of people to people analysis that people garner the use of body language for their benefits. These all terms will be carefully discussed in this book and emphasis will be given to the concept of reading the minds of others.

Chapter 1 Basic Concepts

This chapter will deal with the basic concepts that are affiliated with analyzing people. It will throw light on approaches to human behavior, the definition of human behavior and the prediction of human behavior. The ideas will be coherent in this regard and a lot of emphases will be given to the term human analysis.

Human Behavior

Human behavior has interpreted a kind of behavior in which a human is perceived in a social, economical and logical context. The behavior starts to evolve from babyhood to adolescence and it has many impacts on it. The babyhood method is used to see the nature and nurture of the baby, through which he is able to attain a strong reservation in the prospects of life. The human behavior of youth is dependent on three modes. The first mode if of cultural progression. Under what culture, the human is able to grow and how the culture impacts the gender of the human is all that cultural progression is about. In this phase, the cultural ingredients that are the role of economics, religion, politics and society are carefully discussed. This cultural progression is able to garner most of the capabilities of the people and with the passage of time, the public is able to transform the ideas of human behavior effectively. Therefore, cultural progression is a valid argument, which gives brief institutions to work holistically.

The second mode is cognitive development in which the people are able to be interpreted in the construct of small and large cognition holistically. The cognition comes with respect to time and the person is interpreted according to cognition. This means that more the person thinks, the cognition process wants to be established effectively and with the passage of time, the people are able to have more insight into this respective issue.

So, cognition development is a process through which a person's mind is actually construed and with the process of time and phase, he is understood to be a human.

The third mode is of gender development. By gender development, it is asserted the evolutionary phases, that the person is able to integrate into his or her character through the passage of time, is referred to be as gender development. Gender development is a strong process through which both men and women learn effectively. The men ratio is all about rage and individualistic opinion while the women want to be more progressive and expressive in their nature. Therefore, they tend to mold the constructs of their behavior and with the passage of time, the people are able to have more inclination to the coming time. Thus, the use of gender development is important to be understood in a pragmatic manner.

So, these are three modes of human development and these modes are able to be effective in the coming mode of time due to which they are able to have more generic comprehensions in their making. This concept is more aggressive in its demand and it can demand many overtures in its coming phase.

Theories of Human development

This portion of the chapter will deal strongly with the constructs of human development in which the person is able to have strong modes of comprehension with the public. These theories will be developed by eminent philosophers and scientists in the coming time. The individual that use these kinds of behavior were Sigmund Freud, Charles Darwin and many more. Their theories along with their comprehensions are as follows:

Sigmund believed that every person is born with a notion known as libido. This libido is tantamount to the emotional development of the child and the child is able to harness the emotional development of libido and thus, with the passage of time, he develops the aspirations of love and adoration. The aspiration is more systematic in their nature and the child learns the wrongs and rights of life. This libido makes the child more pragmatic in its nature and the child can delve into many aspirations in later life. The child learns the love matters with the mom of the family, he tends to be more affiliated with the opposite gender and there is a sense of authorization of the person with the family member. Therefore, the construction of libido is a concept, which is more effective for people to learn it holistically. The idea is simple in its regard and hence the people are able to make the inclinations in it with respect to time.

Freud also developed a structure of personality for the people. The people are able to have a strong mode of reservation with the other modes of society. Freud believed that every person has its own sense of longing with other personalities and the personalities change with respect to time. The time of personality development is able to induce people with more and more assertions with respective time. The time table of the person varies with strong conservations and the person is able to have more evolution in the coming time. Therefore, the personality assessment of the person is able to be achieved with respect to time. Freud believed that in order to have a strong goal in personality development, one needs to harbor subjectivity in its core relations. The subjectivity could come with respect to time and the person can learn through it. If the subjectivity is all minimum and the person is not able to have enough interactions with the people then there is no usage of a strong personality. The personality orders will deplete with respect of time and the person would not be able to make hard assertions in the coming time. Thus, the personality assessment needs to be checked while catering to the making of a personality and Freud believes that it is an important way to check the balances of the person in the coming time.

Erick Erikson was also of the belief of how people can be elevated in the construct of emotional belief. He believed that people are able to have sound knowledge on the topic of assertion and personality making. However, the situations in the coming time are quite different. Erik wanted the person to have an emotional check on them through which many people, will be able to have sound careers in the book. The idea is that the person is not able to make sound assertions in the coming time. He believed that the person must have an emotional character making in the time and this will help them to make the issues to make more interesting and capable in the coming time. Therefore, Erick will make you believe that the person will be able to induce more progression in the coming time.

Erik had eight stages of development for the human. These are: infancy, trust versus mistrust, early childhood, preschool and school age. He believed that the person is able to learn a lot through these days and with the passage of time, the person is able to have a strong check on his mind as well. These eight stages govern the body language as well as the human behavior of the individual in a coherent manner. The trust versus mistrust is a mindset and a process in which the child is able to learn the major advantages of socialization and ideas that who to trust and who not to. The trust factor comes with the process of time and it helps the individual to learn many ground realities of the time and human behavior. Therefore, it is important to understand how the public is able to be shamed by the narrative of human development.

Another scientist in this educational venture is Piaget, who belongs to Switzerland and he is able to make the mobilities of the personality a bad place. He wants to study the intellectual functioning and reasoning of the individual that how the person is able to have strong intellectual cognition with a person in an effective manner. The effect of the cognition is so sound and great that the person is able to carve out a personal space of livelihood to other personalities in the coming time. The cognition helps to have a systematic endeavor in the coming time and therefore, a person is able to have a strong impact on its personality with the coming time. Thus, cognition is a side to a person's ability with which he is able to make a strong inclination in the person's mind. Hence, it is important for you to understand that why the person is not able to have a strong grip on intellectual freedom and this is exactly a thesis that Mr. Piaget is able to develop with the passage of time.

Next comes the contextualization of learning theory. This is the theory that advocates the sum of all the construction of humans in the coming time. This theory asserts the possibility of strong cognition and mobility in the coming time and any person, who has a strong sense of living is able to have a concentrated pillar of extractions in the coming time. The learning theory is able to make sound credentials in the coming time. This theory helps individuals to make reasons for living and adopting free in the coming time. The people want to make the credence of the personalities more functioning in the coming time and according to them, the person is able to have a sense of pleasure if all its learning and progression are learned in an effective manner. The idea here is not that the person is not able to make strong contention in the coming time but he is sure of dealing with the person float in an effective manner. This sense of actualization comes in the person when he is learning and hence, learning theory helps to deal with the person more effectively and holistically.

So, these are some of the theories, spearheaded by political scientists that can lead to the comprehension of the public. Human development is a complex manner, which is able to be perceived collectively by humans and humans tend to resolve more contextualization for human development. These theories will help to resolve the function come in a generic way and the person will understand effectively the constructs of the individual in a standard manner. Therefore, human development is a process that is able to have a strong generalization of the instruments in a cool manner. The idea is simply that one needs to be well functioning and adaptable in its current outlook and in order to have more strong ingredients of human development, one also needs to form strong approaches to it. Thus, the next section of the book will deal with the incisive approaches which help us understand the mode of human development easily.

Approaches to Understand Human Behavior

There are five major approaches to understand human behavior.

1. The Psychodynamic Approach

The psychodynamic approach was propounded by Sigmund Freud in which he believed that there are three personalities that develop the approach of the person. One is the development of the illness factor. This factor was discovered in the year 1993, when Freud was able to discuss the advantages of the illness emanating of the child. This theory was further comprehended with the passage of time and the people believed that it was able to make the functionalities of the personality look better. Another theory was about the conscious and the subconscious manner. This theory believed that people are able to delve into the personalities of the person in an effective manner. The conscious mind is the mind that is aware of all the pros and cons of living. Whereas, the subconscious mind is the mind, which heralds some of the important aspirations of daily life. According to Freud, the subconscious mind clearly stores a lot of information in the minds of the public and with the passage of time, the person is able to have a strong version of interest in it. The idea of the construction is quite similar to the game because the psychodynamic approach will give you strong comprehension about the functioning of the mind. The system will thereby make you believe in it and with the passage of time, you will be able to have a stronghold on the construction effectively. Therefore, the psychodynamic approach helps you to psychologically listen to the minds of the people and understand them effectively.

2. Behavioral Approach

This is a kind of approach which makes the behaviors of other people understandable through experiences and external stimulus. By many psychologists it is also referred to as the classical conditioning method and the conditioning is done by altering the external stimulus of the public. The public gets to know the major ingredients of the development of behaviorism and with the passage of time, the people get to know the true nature of all the components of real life. The idea is simple and straight here that to make sure that how the people are able to have more strategic interest in their coming, the behavioral approach is possibly maintained and implemented. Therefore, the behavioral approach is an approach, which needs to be strengthened by all means and it tends to give strong reservations in the coming time. So, the reason for making the humans look more understandable and adjustable, the people must not make the hectic decision of life and try its best in making the reasons go way bound.

Predicting Human Behavior

The human behavior of humans can be predicted in the following ways.

The use of Homecourt

This is the manipulation technique in which the individual uses his or her home as an advantage for his own benefits. The psychological demeanor was used to define the crux of the people, who were under the liability of the people. For the substantiation of this case, it is important to understand that the people, who are in a psychological condition to manipulate others are very smart. The first rule is that the public must come into consideration of the psychological master and then the master will navigate his thoughts. First and foremost, the master uses the court to manipulate the personalities and then the public first advocates the use of manipulation to be just and obscure.

Establishing the stance first and then looking for weaknesses

In the manipulation of psychology, it is important to understand that the establishment of the stance is first. The stance needs to be manifested first and then it is established so that the people, who are listening to the track come under the way of the manipulator. Once the stance of the manipulator is established then the maneuvering is very easy. The people have to understand the use of the stance easily and then they have to use the words of the manipulator as a source of manipulation. The people can easily be thrown into the abyss when the manipulator asks a lot of questions. The idea is that the public first navigates the stance and then the manipulator can use the stance to find its justification. If the manipulator wants to find the essence of the stance and if he finds some distortion of the stance then he can avoid the crux of the stance very badly.

Manipulation of Facts

If you want to assert the significance of the psychology of manipulation, then the facts stated can be used to deceive. The facts can be of any statement and that can be used to defy the logic of the people. For instance, if the manipulator is using the fact sound of one thing then that thing can be used to defy as well. People that can assess the logic of the personalities can manipulate by navigating them through their own lies. This is the act of manipulation if people are using the effects of deviance in an effective manner.

Overwhelming with facts and statistics

First and foremost, the fact and statistics can be used to defy the personalities of the public. The facts are to be constructed in an effective manner so that the manipulator can be used to defy the odds of manipulation. So, for a strong manipulation, you have to overwhelm the facts and statistics with the people. The people can be used to come under the clout of statistics if the public is not able to use a strong mode of psychological messages. Therefore, it is important that psychology can be used to interpret the essence of the public in a logical manner.

Overwhelming with procedures and Red tape

In order to maintain the crux of other personalities, the manipulator uses procedures and red tapes to give more defying reasons to the public. The manipulator will use the procedural versions, in which the public has to be manipulated in a stringent manner. The manipulator can be harnessed in a strong way so that the public can give concrete methods to it. For this reason, to be constructed, the manipulator uses some procedures and advantages through which the normal public comes into oppression. This oppression is used to defy the lands of the public and the public comes under the manipulation of the manipulator. So, in order to manipulate the people, the psychologists can use the crux of procedures and some secretive tapes that can be used in a strong manner.

Raising the voice and Displaying Negative Emotions

The manipulator in order to make the voice of the public effective has to raise the voice of himself. The manipulator uses some strong means and modes through which he is able to forecast a shadow of darkness. This darkness is used to construct the methods of manipulation among the stakeholders and the people can come under effective modes of destruction. Also, the negative emotions, give the value of harsh realities among the public and they get severely neglected by the personalities. Therefore, it is important to understand that the public is not able to get manipulated if they see the raised level of voice and hence there is a display of festering emotions among the people.

Negative Surprises

The negative surprises are another mode of manipulation by the manipulator. The manipulate can be using harsh negative surprises through which the people are not able to understand their nature. These negative surprises also affect the effects of the mentality of the public and with the passage of time, the people do not get easily comfortable in this essence. The negative surprises show a strong moment of disinterest among the public and there is a culture of disassociation among the public through the negative surprises. The negative surprises give a sense of bad omens for the public through which the people are not able to give standard modes of deviation for the public.

Giving you a little or no time to decide

The time that has been given to you is either less time or there is no time. The manipulator wants to get his thing done because only then he is effective in his mode. The manipulator would cast his own means to come in front of the public. The time that has been slotted for the manipulator has a strong version of connectedness with the people and thus, there needs to be a strong sense of affection for the people. Therefore, the time of decision that has been given to you is a tool of the manipulator so that the public is able to give more directions for the public. So, the time has to be a motive interest for the public to understand in an effective manner.

Use of Negative Humor

The negative humor is a manipulating tool to disassociate you from your being. The manipulator would cast negative humor on you and will do his best to make you feel bad about the situation. This manipulation is further designed by the manipulator to disempower you and with its continuous bolstering, the use of negative humor could be very harsh and brutal for you. Therefore, the use of negative humor could be used to induce isolationism and fanaticism in public and could be very pernicious for you as well. If the use of negative humor could be bad for you then manipulation could be a stringent maneuver to showcase in-effectiveness among you.

Consistent Judgement

The consistent judgment could be a harsh tactic to induce fright among you. The manipulator could use the essence of judgement to make you feel discomfort able.

How it can be done? This is as follows: Suppose, you are sitting in a room and the manipulator is sitting in front of you and you are able to hear the statements of the manipulator and with the passage of time, the public is not able to define the essence of the judgments properly. The public is quite effective in harboring the essence of the manipulator and if the manipulator is successful is dissing you with his judgments then finally you are under his claw. The consistent judgment will make you feel very demotivated and with the passage of time, you will be feeling delusional.

Silent Treatments

When the manipulator wants to harbor his mechanism then he uses the edifice of silence. This silence is very haunting. It is very managerial and with the passage of time, it induces a bad version of manipulation among you. You get affected by the silence of the manipulator and in time, this becomes very pestering among you. The silent treatment is also very haunting at an individualistic level because at times, the public is not able to see the results of it in a discomforting manner. Therefore, silent treatments can be used to haunt the premises of the individual in a bad manner.

Thus, these are some of the mechanisms that make the prediction of human behavior look way too easy. Therefore, human development needs to be adopted with the passage of time properly.

Chapter 2 Body Language

This chapter will give heed to the concept of body language. The important contents along with their clarifications are as follows:

Importance of Body Language

The body language gives you strong commitments and strong waves of confidence in you. The following are some of the ways that can make body language important for you.

Body Language can generate compassion for you

Just imagine that your shoulders are way too back, the smiles are apparent on your face, the stomach in of yours and the strong eye contact; all these features are important for you and with the passage of time, you will realize that you will be able to induce a spirit of confidence in you and with this confidence, you can make a lot of efforts to the human development and can make the analysis an important way for the public to come on. Therefore, body language can generate compassion for you.

Hand gestures representing yourself

In anybody's language, the use of hand gestures is able to give a sounding impact to the listeners. With strong gestures, the people are able to have pertinent soundings in their constructs and the people are able to infuse meticulous planning in their formation. The idea is simple in this sense because the more you use hand gestures, the more you are able to make healthy developments in the scenario. Therefore, hand gestures are an important tool for you to use in a conversation.

Having a sustainable conversation

The more you use actions in a body language with your tongue and body, the more sustainable conversation you will intend to have. It depends on what is the mechanism of the body language and how this mechanism is able to make you different in any conversation. If you are shy and a little hysterical while conversing, then the conversation would not last long. However, if you tend to be a little more convincing then the conversation will last for long. The idea is simply that you need to have a strong momentum of conversation in your dialogue and with the passage of time, you will develop yourself much better. Hence, the importance of body language is all reflected in your domains in the coming time.

Have an open posture

The use of an open posture is a tool to construct the language portion of the personality. It gives its importance in the construction of humble words and you must be able to have an open posture while you are making yourself more confident and reliable in any conversation. The more you are able to have an open posture, the more you can seduce the personalities with your body language. Therefore, before speaking always have an open posture, due to which you will be able to be joined by other people effectively. Hence, the idea of an open posture starts with strong conversation and impact and you are able to make stringent mechanisms in time.

Speaking without Words

This part of the chapter will tell you that your postures and eye contacts can speak effectively and proverbially for others while you are about to start a conversation. It has the following contents of its clarification.

The use of firm handshake

The more firm is your handshake, the more impact you are able to give to the audience or the people with whom you want to speak. The people judge your mentality when they shake hands with you and they are able to perceive you directly once you are able to have proper handshaking with your friends.

For instance, you want to a bar, the friends at their have a token of interest for you and they tend to give you strong assertions before a conversation. In such a situation, it is quite better to have a strong mode of conversation with the use of a firm handshake. This gesture will deploy hundreds of ways to make you feel much better and proactive in the coming time. Therefore, it is always important to start a conversation with someone, using a handshake.

Maintaining good eye contact

The maintenance of good eye contact is another strong feature of you to make good eye contact. It is not necessary that you are not speaking with anyone but it is highly important for you to have stern contact with others while having a conversation. This gesture would seem as if you are able to give a sound impact on your conversation without talking.

Avoiding touching your face

If you want to speak without words then do avoid your face while having a conversation. The idea of avoidance comes with time and you need to avoid other properly if you believe that you can make a strong impact on others life. Therefore, while you are able to have a strong impact of conversation try your best in making the lives of others way too better and you can do this while knowing how to avoid touching others' faces. Thus, the very way to make others avoid your face is by listening to the true alternates of your life and with the passage of time, you will have a strong impact on your conversation.

The morals of Public speaking

If you want to speak gently in front of the public then learn to speak to the inner thoughts of yourself. This means that you have to be very gentle and firm in your league and with the passage of time, you will understand how public speaking can be done more effectively. Therefore, the very idea of public speaking comes with time and in order to make the public a better place, you have to convey the idea in a much better and positive manner. Therefore, the morals of public speaking are everything that you need to know while you are speaking.

How body Language works

There is a strong saying that you cannot hide your lying eyes. The eyes of you are so intact while you are speaking and the body language that is used for this purpose is further augmented if you are able to have better results in the following. Body language works by making the eyes, the shoulders, the facial expressions and the saying tactics in a strong manner holistically. Therefore, body language comes with the passage of time and it works if you are smart in conversation, precise to the topic and relevant in the mode of comprehension. This is how the body language of the citizen properly.

Decoding Body Language

Body language can be decoded by using the following aspects of the conversation.

Facial Expressions

Body language can be easily assessed if one is able to recognize the facial expressions of others and while doing so. The facial expressions give a lot of consensus making while they are able to give solid expressions in the coming time. These facial expressions are a must to be used in the coming time and if one has to deploy strong expressions in his demand then all these things need to be employed pragmatically.

Body Proxemics

Body Proxemics is a way to up bring the closeness in a person and it is regarded as the best way to decode someone's body language. If you are new in the decoding business then you must harbor the use of body proxemics in your daily life. This concept will make the body straighten up in a close manner and with the passage of time, it will be uploaded in a frank manner. Therefore, body proxemics will let the decoding of the body language function in a better way.

Ornaments

If the person has worn some ornaments then the ornaments will help you understand the body language of that person in an effective manner. For instance, if there are some bands and chains on the human body then such ornaments depict the pluralist nature of the individual. Similarly, the makeup on the individual will set the human respect affect in a perpetual manner. Therefore, ornaments have a strong version of intellect in the person's body effectively.

Easily Read Body Language

This portion will deal with the argument about how language is properly instructed and easily read.

Study the eyes

If you are listening to somebody then carefully understand the body language of the individual. The eyes give you the strong reservation of the personality and with the passage of time, one is able to manifest strong feelings of the people in the coming time. Therefore, the eyes of the public are the reflection of the people and with the passage of time, you are able to induce strong commitments to the people.

Gaze at the face

You have to gaze at the face of the individual to know that if he is fine or not. This mode of interpretation will make you get a lot of respect in the facial expression. The gazing of the face is an important mode of understanding the person and with the passage of time, the person will get more understanding of the personality. Therefore, the gazing at the face is an important way to make things a little better and to decode the body language of a person effectively.

See if the person is mirroring you

The person, who is able to mirror you effectively will make the expression of the face in a pertinent manner. The person, who is mirroring you is able to read the minds and expressions of the person and with the passage of time, the person has many agitations in the coming time. The person that is able to induce mirroring in the person's mind will be able to give strong agitation in the coming time. Therefore, the person needs some of the socializing manners in it due to which it is able to induce frustration in the coming.

Observe the head movement

Observing the head movement will make you realize that the head of the person is something that will make the situation look more difficult and agitated in its construct. The observance of the head is as strong as it is perceived by the individual and with the passage of time, the person is able to give more and more agitation in the coming time. Therefore, the observance of the head movement is as crucial and cruel in its nature and that can lead to a strong mode of disturbance in the coming time.

Watch for the hand's signals

The person's hand signals are those signals that make the person look more agitative and frustrated in the coming time. The person can do a lot of socialization when he is able to do hand signals and use them reflectively in the coming. The shaking of the person's mind can lead to a strong agitation in the coming time and the watch can retain a lot for the individuals in the coming time. Therefore, the watch of the hand's signals can lead to strong construction in the coming time and this could be very effective in the coming time.

Examine the position of the arms

The position of the arms can be selected for the better nourishment of the people. If the person is able to do a better examination of the position of arms then he is able to read the body language of the person in an effective manner. The examination of the position of the arms can unfold many realizations of the person and the person is able to manifest the minds of others in a humble way. Therefore, the examination of the position of arms can reflect the body language of the person in an effective manner and in order to understand the person's mind, the man will able to reflect the nourishment of the women in a pertinent manner.

How to read your own body language

This portion of the chapter will look into the consideration of reading the language of the other personality.

Seeing the mirror and observing your acute expressions

If you want to observe the body language of yourself then see the expression of yourself in the mirror. With the passage of time, the person will give you a lot of concentration and you will come to know a lot of assertion in the coming time. You will come to realize that you have some other aspects of yourself and with the passage of time, you will decode your own body language. The crossed legs and the strong eye set depict that you are not in the mood of others to watch you. The seeing of the mirror and the observance of acute expression will provide a lot of assertions in the coming time.

Therefore, the more you look into the mirror, the more you are able to have a better understanding of yourself in the coming time.

Chapter 3 How to read people

Reading people is another way of making the people think about themselves and with the passage of time, the people admire such qualities. The contents of this chapter are as follows:

Considerations about reading people's mind

1. Isolation

Isolation starts with the basics of brainwashing. The brainwashing is important to understand by the manipulator. The manipulator would use the edifice of isolation. The isolation is effective in its use and by all means necessary, the manipulator tends to isolate you from the social order. He makes you understand that the world is not effective in its use and can be very haunting in its meaning. Therefore, isolation is a technique used to be understood effectively.

2. Attacks on self-esteem

While brainwashing, the manipulator uses the
edifice of attacks on self-esteem. For him, the
brain of you is of high importance. Whatever
he thinks of you can be altered only if he
wishes to change your brain. You will make
the self-esteem of yourself and by the
prospects you will understand that the
manipulator is using this edifice to brainwash
you.

3. Mental abuse

In order for the brainwashing to work more
effectively, the use of mental abuse is of high
importance. The use of mental abuse will
work in a practical manner and will thwart the
conformity of the brain precisely. The mental
abuse can be used of mentality and effectively
and with the passage of time, you will
understand that you are seeking to feel very
obscene. Therefore, the crux of mental abuse
will be effective for you in its making.

4. Physical abuse

The physical abuse will look into the brainwashing in a complete manner. Do your best to avoid the physical abuse of the manipulators. Otherwise, you will find yourself in a turbulent manner. The physical abuse can lead to the tarnishing of the brain and you will feel very bad at the end. Therefore, the concept of physical abuse must never be allowed to be furnished in the first place.

5. Only allowing contact with selected members

Brainwashers or manipulators want you to contact with selected members. The selected members will cater to the brainwashing effectively and with the passage of time, they can be successful if you do not object them in the first place. The selected members will showcase a culture of degeneration among you and with the passage of time, you will feel very bad and bodacious. Therefore, the contact hearing is only important for you if you wish to understand the nature of the selected members.

6. Us versus them

This slogan will make you understand that the entire slogan of unity will forever haunt you. The brainwashing gets its momentum when it is trending at a larger scale and there is a policy of us contamination with them syndrome. This means that the US is not able to engage them processors and with the passage of time, the people are able to have a strong fan page about it.

7. Lie less and do more

The deceiving personality knows that he has to make sure of his conversations. If he lies more and more then he will get under the curve of badness and with the passage of time, he will feel himself to be bad. Also, there is a chance of him to get caught and could end himself in a bad manner.

Therefore, in deception, the manipulator lies less and less and gets away from it.

8. Telling the truth in a misleading manner

Telling the truth in a misleading manner means that one has to be very effective in its regard. The telling of truth in a misleading manner showcases the strength of personalities and hence, the people are able to be maneuvered in a better way. Therefore, the deceiving personality uses the edifice of deception to make sure that the individual is all bad and worse in the frame.

9. The deceiver knows his target

The deceiver always does his best in knowing the target in an effective manner and when he approaches in an acute way, he tends to be very effective and efficacious in its rating. Therefore, the use of deception is a tool to know the target effectively and the time taken for its progress will also be used in a longer way.

10. Keep your facts straight

The keeping of facts straight makes you understand what are the uses of fact measures. The idea is simply that the deceiving personality uses the facts straight and effective in its regard and with the passage of time, the facts are quite pertinent in its regard. Therefore, the keeping of facts means that the person is able to have a strong version of manipulation in him.

11. Staying Focused

The idea of staying focused is that the art of deception requires stealth and help. The stealth requires strong focus and assertion and with the passage of time, the man has to be very strong and sturdy in its manner. The focus paradigm will come in its manner and hence, the person is able to have a core function of its people.

12. Watch your signals

The people are able to have a strong set of affection for themselves. The idea is simply that the deceiving personality will focus on the coming signals and with the passage of time, the personality will do its best in making the game more astute and effective. Therefore, the idea is simple for the psychologist and the manipulator to handle.

13. Always turn up the pressure

Turning up the pressure will always make the people look more and more agile. The pressure comes with a stringent mode of affection and with the passage of time, the manipulator makes it look easier and more effective. Therefore, the use of pressure can ease the process in a curbing manner and thus, the deception will make the process more and more great.

Techniques to read easily people

1. Do all the thinking

The manipulators will do their best in doing the thinking for you. They will think for you and will tell you the best for you. However, doing revolves around the crux of manipulation. They are doing this so that you can be in their domain and thus, there mind control tactic is successful. This is the better prospect for you and once you do this, you are in the action of the mind control.

2. Starting an avalanche

The avalanche is a marketing firm that makes you strong and subtle in their regard. The creation of an avalanche is pertinent for you to understand and with the passage of time, there is secret maneuvering for you and you will induce an avalanche for you. The avalanche for you is that you have to be in the claws of an avalanche for you. Therefore, the mindset of the individual is easily dodging and with the passage of time, he is able to have control of the manipulator.

3. Ask for an inch take a mile

The asking for an inch and taking a mile is a concept that asserts the importance of taking things quickly. This means that the manipulator would cast a shadow quickly and with the passage of time, he would ask things for you which would have no actual reasons. This can be explained with an example. The manipulator would do a big favor for you and in return, you would love to comply with him and with the passage of time, the manipulator would not take your compliments. He would ask of something great and then he would take a profuse amount. This is the basic tenant of manipulation that asks something else and gets an all-in return.

4. Always have a real deadline

The real deadline means that the person has to realistically forecast a shadow line on you and you are not expected to do anything in return. The deadline means that you will do something for him and in return, he will give you proper isolation for you. Therefore, it is important to understand the nature of you and you will have the prospects in no time. The real deadline refers to the last concept of the material and with the passage of time, you will get a new result in the formation.

5. Giving ten times more

The manipulator will be able to leverage himself by giving you more and more things. If he does something for you and in return you do better for him. Then this is the mode of affection for him. Therefore, the giving of ten-time will provide you a sustainable moment of affection for yourself. This is exactly the method of utilization for you and you will be able to have more relaxation of it. Therefore, the giving of more things is actually a way to control the minds of the public and he will get more and more insight into it. Thus, the giving of more and more things will provide you with better affection.

6. Standing for something greater for you

The people are able to get in your mind control if they believe in you. In order for them to believe in you, you have to do something great for them. To an extent, that they will always recall of you while they are pursuing something and they are able to have a problem in any situation. In this way, they will harbor all the mechanisms for you that will induce a great sense of affection for you. Therefore, standing for something is actually an act of affection for you and the people around you.

7. Be shameless

The people are always shameless, who want to manipulate you carefully. They feel as it is their importance to have you onboard for their progression. They believe that people will understand you effectively if they are shameless. Being shameless does not mean that they dance in all nudity for you but in actual terms, they are able to have a strong sense of affection for you. Therefore, being shameless is an attribute to you so that you are able to have a precautionary sense of affection in you.

8. Eye seduction

In psychology, you can use the edifice of eye to eye connection in order to make the eyes look greater and more effective. The eye effect is important to seduce the other end of personalities. The personalities are able to have a great sense of seduction in them due to which the public is able to have fun and persuasion. The eye seduction is tantamount to give more and more value to the psychologists and in time, they are able to have more fun and zeal in eye seduction. Thus, it is important to do eye seduction in the coming time.

9. Using the lack nesses

In dark psychology, you can use the lack of nesses of other personalities so that you can have leverage on other personalities. You will understand in time that the individuals will be able to have more and more zeal in them. The lack of nesses can give you more aspects of their clout. The clout can be more incisive in their regard. The use of edifice can help you give more and more aspiration in the coming. The psychologist and the manipulator will use this prospect to gain leverage in the coming time.

Tricks for reading people's thoughts

1. He is charming and nice

The manipulator is all charm and nice at first. He would try his best in making you feel comfortable and gradually, he would impart his shrewdness. First, he would come in your comfort zone by wishing you birthdays, by giving you gifts and making you feel less agitated about anything then he would cast his dogmas. Once he knows that you will not bother him about anything then he would tell you to do anything by all means necessary. Sometimes, his manipulation is so strong and stringent that he can make you do anything even murder. Thus, this is the idea of manipulation that is started with charming voices and ending in catastrophe. Beware of such people.

2. Denial

The manipulator would always deny any assertion or statement of guilty on him. He would be felt exempt from any charges and would dare to see himself in the crux of any problem. If you somehow even manage to bring him in any disaster then he would just simply run away and would assert his innocence overcharges. He would think of himself as a strong mode of eccentricity and he would deny any kind of charges on him and would plead his innocence all over time. This is the true nature of denial that it tends to be very compulsive and bad in its progression and becomes haunting as well. Therefore, the denial is able to make the people look very bad and obsolete to the individual.

3. Lying

The people are able to lie a lot and those, who can actually conform themselves on it are lying. The lying edifice starts with the inculcation of hate speech and derogation and with the passage of time, the people tend to learn a lot of lying. The innocents are not able to see the manifestation of lying in their inner sides and they do not how exactly is the platform of lying quite degenerate about it. The lying helps the manipulator to learn more and more about the advances of the individual and with the passage of time, he comes one step closer tin dodging and abhorring you. This is the strong crux of lying that needs to be strengthened by all means necessary.

4. Excessive Flattery

This sign is of huge importance to the manipulator. The manipulator is able to do a lot of flattery for the individuals and with the passage of time, the individual can harbor flattery and sweetness among the individuals. The flattery helps to manipulate the individuals in a strong manner and this flattery can be of any side and sustenance. The idea exhibited here is quite strong as the people are able to create an environment of justice and order in the citizens and the flattery helps to regulate themselves in an effective manner.

5. Forced Teaming

The individual can use the teaming of the layers for his own motives. This teaming can be devious in its nature and can reflect many ills and whims of the societies. The teaming can also lead to social segregation in society and with the passage of time, the person can easily regulate its crux in a mature manner. The force teaming can appoint strong versions of impact for the students and with the passage of time, the individuals can come up with strong assertions. The forced teaming could be the use of any strength and value and it could be very destructive in its nature as well. Therefore, forced teaming is a sign of affection for the manipulator and it is destruction for the students as well.

6. Good First Impression

The manipulator will always do his best to make the best impression that he can in order to carefully influence the minds of other people. This is a well-managed task just to make sure that the audience is under the reflection of the manipulator and you will all mean necessary, follow under the trap of the manipulators. The good impression can be very expressive in its command and it can yield to proper potential as well but its lasting impacts are very pernicious. With the subtle use of a good impression, the person can easily establish his core links with you and can make you do almost everything. Therefore, a person having an expression of a good impression in him will be interpreted as a manipulator.

7. Pretending to be a victim

The manipulator is of a harsh and smart demeanor. He knows that if he pretends to be a victim then all the people will listen to him and no matter what are the conditions his stance and statements will stand correct. He will understand this assertion in a jiffy and will do his best to make the public very bad and obscene. The idea is simply that the person is not able to convey his true propositions to the public and he pretends to be a victim. The concept of victimhood tarnishes his image and with the passage of time, he tends to deviate from the straight path. This mere concept completely obstructs the use of empathy from the manipulator's mind and with the passage of time, he feels very degenerative. Therefore, the person, who is a manipulator, will always have a sign of victimhood in him.

8. Silent Treatment

This sign is of strong admiration in the person, who is playing to be a manipulator. The manipulator will easily treat the level of punishment to the audience and while doing this, he will be silent and stringent as hell. This is the idea of concealing and secrecy that the manipulator employees and with the passage of time, he is able to impart a devious mechanism of dealing with things upon the individual. Therefore, it is important to observe the silent treatment of things in the public and this silent treatment will actually make the person feel very atrocious. Therefore, in order to see the sign of manipulation the person has to be very silent and if he is found silent then yes, he is a manipulator.

9. Appearing to be selfless

The signs of selflessness are the signs that make the individual look very harsh and strong. The selflessness comes in the individuals either he has a golden heart or is he using the emblem of selflessness for himself. For instance, a boy, who is a manipulator falls in love with a person and asserts her to be selfless. At the moment, perhaps he is vouching for a love affair but in the true sense, he tends to be manipulative. He would cast the shadow of badness upon the girl just to have an advantage of her and even get something from her. Therefore, the use of selflessness is also a quality that needs to be strengthened properly.

10. Guilt Tripping

The idea of guilt-tripping is essential to understand as to decipher the nature of manipulation. In the guilt-tripping, the manipulator harbors the power of guilt in an individual and with the passage of time, he manipulates the other individual uses his guilt. He showcases that he is no the one, which is guilty and he trips the momentary aspects of guilt just to convey his innocence. This is a culture of guilt-tripping and it is easily found in all the corners of the world. Even international leaders use the edifice of guilt-tripping to transcend a culture of guilt-tripping. Therefore, it is important to understand that guilt-tripping can lead to a devastating blow of injuries and badness.

11. Shaming

When the manipulator easily acquires his motives, he starts shaming others. He feels that the individual is of no worth and in order to destroy him completely, he must be shamed. He would shame you using harsh means, he would kill you possibly, he would employ derogatory remarks upon you and he would instill a culture of deviance among you.

Therefore, the culture of shaming is found prevalent among the manipulators and if one has to recognize a manipulator, then he can use this edifice for good reasons. This is the revering identity of the individuals by all means necessary.

12. Intimidation

The person is able to intimidate the other personality if he is manipulative. The manipulation is a hectic task as it requires a lot of effort for the manipulator to intimidate you. This intimidation can be strong as it could lead to an effective mode of manipulation for the individuals. The intimidation starts with a turning point as it will create more efflux of opportunities for the personalities for you. This culture of intimidation is great as you can create more manipulative tactics for your self but in the end, it will be harsh for you. Therefore, it is mandatory to understand that intimidation is a recognizing aspect of a manipulator.

13. Diversion

Diversion refers to the diversity of opinion among the manipulators so that the people can easily lead to a better productive scenario of people to people contact. This diversity is important for you as it will yield a greater sense of affection for you and in the presence of time, you will be able to diversify your opinion based on a common strand of diversity. This means that the manipulator can use the edifice of diversity just to yield more manipulation and strength in him. This can be taken in the aspect of the plurality of opinion and in many ways, it can be dangerous as well.

Tips for reading people

The following are the ways of reading people.

Creation of a baseline

Creation of a baseline means that a person's identity is subjected. The baseline of the person is very good to interpret in the minds of the people and with the passage of time, the baseline is subjected to a powerful construct of happenings. These happenings will let to a better possibility of reading that person in a coherent manner and the creation of a baseline will help you understand the cognition of a person in a better way.

Look for deviations

Deviations mean that the person is not able to find strong connections of the person and the person is not able to create better complacency of the people in their lead. The look for deviation is an interim world, where the people are able to have strong connections in the coming. So, if you want to look in the world and see that the person is able to create some reflections in the past then see how he deviates in daily life. This is called the process of deviations, which imbue a process of agitation in the person for a longer run.

Compare and Contrast

You need to compare and contrast with the person with whom you want to be settled in the coming time. The comparison comes with the systematic evaluation of the process of the people and the people are able to have strong endurance about it. The contrasting factors come with respect to time and the people are able to create strong reservations about it. Therefore, the reservation that come through it will have comparison and contrast about it in the coming time.

Identify the strong voice

Identification of a strong voice is an important tool, which makes life easier with the process of socialization. The identification leads to the belief that the person having a strong voice will eventually create more tendencies in the coming. The strong voices will generate compassion in its life and with the passage of time, the people are able to store an identification of the socialized person. Therefore, the identification of a strong voice leads to a better way of understanding things effectively.

Pinpoint action words

Pinpointing action words means that you are able to have better decoding of the language in you with a better amount of time. The pinpointing of action means that the more you have a better reaction of the words, the more you have strong connections in it. The action words come with strong use of words and within time, you are able to have a better understanding of the person in the random list. So, do your best in pinpointing the action in people's lives if you want to make a better understanding of the people.

Look for personality clues

Try your best to make the best of the personality of yourself and try to look for more clues in the personality of others if you are willing to make new changes in the coming life. The personality clues come with a respected amount of time and you are able to induce better skeptics in the person for a longer duration of time. The look is a secret way for other personalities to understand the better way of indulging the rights of personalities in the coming time. Therefore, it is important to look for more options in a person and with the amount of coming time, the person is able to make better administration in the coming time. Thus, the possibility of clues is a better way to make things more pragmatic in the coming time and hence there is a lot of understanding, which can be helpful in the better running of time.

Gestures for interpreting people

They are many gestures through which many people can be interpreted. The following are some of the examples.

Standing with hands-on-hips

Standing with hands-on-hips is a strong assertive tone through which the person is able to have an impact of strength and quality. The person feels that the more he is acting like this, the more he is able to have better projections in life. The assertiveness comes with the time of strong critique and impact through which he is able to give out a bad manner in this regard. Standing with hands-on-hips is also a way of inducing strength and valor to the people.

Standing with legs crossed

Standing with legs crossed means that the person is able to induce submission and subtleness in the manner. The standing with legs crossed comes with the passage of time and the person is able to give a very submissive narrative in this regard. The standing with legs crossed is a reflection to a better mode of reflection to a person and this reflection helps to be sustained in a strong reflection of a person. Hence, standing with legs crossed is a hectic way of leading things in a better mode.

Standing with legs Uncrossed

Standing with legs uncrossed is a mode of reflection and collectiveness. The uncrossed legs marks optimism in a person and the person is able to induce better projections in the other person's mind. The mind of the person is so effective and leading that the person must contain strong emblems of optimism and co-relation in it. The standings come with a perpetual mode of affection in it and the person gives strong efforts of coordination to the person. Therefore, standing with legs uncrossed is a sign of better relief to a person and the person is able to deal with the person's mind collectively.

Touching or playing with hair

This is a sign that the person is not able to pay proper attention to another person holistically. The person, who is touching or playing with hair is a person that has a lot going on in his mind. He is a person with whom you want to have a strong chit chat about everything and you are able to induce a small set of capabilities in him. This person is very logical and effective in his brain and with the passage of time, he wants to deem better ways of understanding in the coming time.

The cowboy stance

This is a stance that is of a cowboy meaning. This means that you are not able to make better understandings of things and perhaps, the person is able to induce a better piece of understanding in the meantime. The cowboy stance is a stance that makes things look in a better way and there is a minor of complication that evolves around the concept of clarity in it. The cowboy stance is a stance that will help you look greater and more effective in the coming time. The stance is a strength of a person and the person is able to give the last impact of things in the coming time. The cowboy stance creates a better way of nourishment for a person and the person is able to have a strong impact on it in the coming time.

Covering the mouth

This is a person, who is very secretive in nature. He likes to talk about things as it is very bad in its construct. The constructs of the mouth are so great in its usage that the person can learn about skeptics and secrecy. Therefore, the covering of the mouth is a mouthpiece for secrecy and a person is able to commit a lot of ways to make sure that the person is about to induce clandestine nature in it. Thus, the use of covering the mouth is a better way to make things appear on the bright side.

Crossed Arms

It is an attitude that solidifies the crossing of a person in a perfect manner. The crossed arms gesture shows that the person is able to make the things go in a positive manner. The positive manner of a person is quite skeptical in this regard as well. The crossed arms help you to maintain better prospects in a person's mind and with the passage of time, the crossed arms will make a hefty price of installments in the coming time. Therefore, the crossed arms will give you a better way to understand things in a positive manner.

Chapter 4 How to detect lies

Lying is an obscene habit and it is used to detect the badness in a person and it should be made clear here that this book will look into the ways of detecting lies and bad qualities.

Chapter 4 How to Detect Lies

Verbal signs of Lying

A person who does the following things to you is actually lying and behaving in a belligerent manner.

1. Do all the thinking

The manipulators will do their best in doing the thinking for you. They will think for you and will tell you the best for you. However, doing revolves around the crux of manipulation. They are doing this so that you can be in their domain and thus, there mind control tactic is successful. This is the better prospect for you and once you do this, you are in the action of the mind control.

2. Starting an avalanche

The avalanche is a marketing firm that makes you strong and subtle in their regard. The creation of an avalanche is pertinent for you to understand and with the passage of time, there is secret maneuvering for you and you will induce an avalanche for you. The avalanche for you is that you have to be in the claws of an avalanche for you. Therefore, the mindset of the individual is easily dodging and with the passage of time, he is able to have control of the manipulator.

3. Ask for an inch take a mile

The asking for an inch and taking a mile is a concept that asserts the importance of taking things quickly. This means that the manipulator would cast a shadow quickly and with the passage of time, he would ask things for you which would have no actual reasons. This can be explained with an example. The manipulator would do a big favor for you and in return, you would love to comply with him and with the passage of time, the manipulator would not take your compliments. He would ask of something great and then he would take a profuse amount. This is the basic tenant of manipulation that asks something else and gets an all-in return.

4. Always have a real deadline

The real deadline means that the person has to realistically forecast a shadow line on you and you are not expected to do anything in return. The deadline means that you will do something for him and in return, he will give you proper isolation for you. Therefore, it is important to understand the nature of you and you will have the prospects in no time. The real deadline refers to the last concept of the material and with the passage of time, you will get a new result in the formation.

5. Giving ten times more

The manipulator will be able to leverage himself by giving you more and more things. If he does something for you and in return you do better for him. Then this is the mode of affection for him. Therefore, the giving of ten-time will provide you a sustainable moment of affection for yourself. This is exactly the method of utilization for you and you will be able to have more relaxation of it. Therefore, the giving of more things is actually a way to control the minds of the public and he will get more and more insight into it. Thus, the giving of more and more things will provide you with better affection.

6. Standing for something greater for you

The people are able to get in your mind control if they believe in you. In order for them to believe in you, you have to do something great for them. To an extent, that they will always recall of you while they are pursuing something and they are able to have a problem in any situation. In this way, they will harbor all the mechanisms for you that will induce a great sense of affection for you. Therefore, standing for something is actually an act of affection for you and the people around you.

7. Be shameless

The people are always shameless, who want to manipulate you carefully. They feel as it is their importance to have you onboard for their progression. They believe that people will understand you effectively if they are shameless. Being shameless does not mean that they dance in all nudity for you but in actual terms, they are able to have a strong sense of affection for you. Therefore, being shameless is an attribute to you so that you are able to have a precautionary sense of affection in you.

Tips for detecting lies in verbal discussion

You must have the following tactics in you to detect lies in any particular verbal discussion.

1. Repression

Repression means that you are about to forget the evil thoughts and mechanisms that could trigger agitation in you. You have to induce the spirit of repression in you so that you may able to forget all the bad thoughts and ideas that one has induced in you. You have to use the concept of acceptance and individualistic effort on you and therefore, you are able to have a stronger version of acceptance in you. Thus, repression acts as a strong defense mechanism and you are able to give viable justifications to it.

2. Projection

In this kind of a mental defense system, you have to project the positive feelings of any problem in front of you. You have to make sure that any negativity that comes into your mind is easily removed and you are able to have a solid grip on your comfortability of the thoughts. You need to make sure that any such ingredients that tend to distort your inner feelings are not hampered and are not projected in your mind. Therefore, the very idea of projecting good feelings in situations of bad feelings is named as projection. Thus, you need to govern these instruments effectively in the manner.

3. Displacement

Displacement means that you need to empower the inner thoughts of yourself in an effective manner and by any yardstick, you need to be pragmatic in the developments. The displacement helps you to engage others in a positive manner and you are able to have a sound impression of yourself. However, if you are not able to make a strong displacement of yourself then you are in the impression of the bad ones. Therefore, displacement helps you make the assertions come in an effective manner.

4. Rationalization

The rationalization mechanism works with the implementation of this principle that you need to come up with strong emotions in your brain. You can avoid any negativity in the atmosphere and most importantly, you cannot sustain without them either. You have to bolster rationalization in yourself so that you are able to have a sustainable feature of intellect in you. You need certain primaries in yourself while you are rationalizing. You have to be bold and independent in your saying and never let lose in front of others no matter what happens. Therefore, rationalization is a strong defense system that makes you believe in your self and no matter where you go, you are able to have a strong system of catering emotions through it.

5. Reaction Formation

The reaction formation is a concept, which indicates that once the negativity has been uttered upon you, you are able to form a reaction on it. The reaction is that you do not need to have a strong reservation about it but you must have the credibility of conjunction in you. The easiest way for you to form a reaction formation is that you need to believe in the formation of strong reactions. You can do them anytime in the coming time and you do not have to feel submerged while doing so. Therefore, the formation of reaction creation is another way to make way for strong opponents coming in the time.

6. Denial

In order to make the emotional mechanism of yourself up to date, you need to deny any such restrictions upon you and must do your best in denying any sort of imposition upon your character. For instance, if someone is imposing any alleged mark on you then you have to make the substance of the world in a reactive manner and must not upbring the concepts of the loser in a bad way. Thus, the denying process is the process that cultivates emotional uprising in you and in order to make, the world a better place, you need to deny any such impositions on you.

Tips for detecting lies in body language

There are six ways of detecting a liar in an acute manner.

Always ask neutral questions

Neutral questions mean that the person is able to ask many neutral questions that tend to derail the motion of the public in an acute manner. The people, who are able to mark black tendencies in public can do it very well. The process is very easy as it involves the powerful use of neutral skepticism and the person is able to have a better mode of understanding in the clear matter. The asking of neutral questions will ultimately lead you to the wrong place and you will come up with hectic assertions in a coming manner. Therefore, asking neutral questions will ultimately lead to the detection of lies.

Find the hot spot

The idea of a hot spot means that there is always a bad ending of a conversation through which a person is able to make bad impressions in the coming time. The hot spot is sometimes a bad way to make things go in a wrong manner. The hot spot of the construction comes with time and the person is able to do bad ways of engulfing things in a wrong manner. The hot spot is a way through which a person gets a lot of understanding in him and hence with the perpetual manner of finding the hot spot, he is able to do things wrong and obscene.

Watch Body language

If you want to detect the scheme of body language then ultimately you will come to this conclusion that how body language will make things work in an effective manner. The body language is a concept, which needs to be carefully understood with a person and with the passage of time, body language tends to deviate with the prospects of time. Therefore, body language is a sort of mode of conviction where one is able to have better understandings of others. Therefore, body language is a careful token which needs to be understood properly in order to have a better formation of lie detection.

Observe micro-facial expressions

The micro facial expression means that you are able to have a strong mode of lie detection in you and you are able to contain a strong sense of affection in you. The use of micro-facial expression will clearly lead you to a better manner and with the passage of time, you will understand how things unfold in a better yet sustainable option. Therefore, the use of micro facial expressions is a concept, which helps you to contain a strong facial mode of expression within you. Thus, the overall use of body language will make the individual affect the rate of things goes in a better way.

Listen to tone, cadence and structure

The listening to tone, cadence and structure is a way through which the person is able to detect lies in an effective manner. Whenever there is a discussion coming in the time, try your best to carefully observing the structure of language if you are able to have it. Understand that you are able to lead the psyche of the individuals carefully with the advent of time and thus, this is a better way of understanding things in a holistic manner. This is a way of making things float so that the person is able to have a better mode of aspiration in the longer run. So, cadence and structure can help things go in a positive manner.

Tips for detecting lies with intuition

Try to use the following gestures in order to form the detection in lied within an intuition.

1. Gaslighting

This is the technique that is used to see if the person's words sound like his actions or not. The gaslighting is a method that can be used to question the belief of the personality and with the passage of time, the person has to understand the use of this tool to use the manipulation effectively. There is a set of questions among the public, used by the manipulator to dodge the essence of the questions and with the passage of time, the entire scenario of the public changes with time all because of the gas questions, asked by the manipulator.

2. Generalizations

The generalizations of a manipulator are a strong sense of demotivation for the public to withstand. The manipulator easily generalizes all the terms and tactics that are employed on a social, economic and political factor and with the passage of time, the generalizations come with time. The generalizations are important enough for a manipulator for the student to understand the essence of all compatible reasons for the public and with the passage of time, the manipulator is able to see the distance of the public go far away. Therefore, the distance of the public from the real cause actually defines the status of the manipulator and the manipulator can control a lot of sense through it. Therefore, the use of a generalizing matter creates more and more aspect for the students and civilians. Thus, the use of generalization gives impetus to the manipulator and with the passage of time, it can be more asserted in the coming. So, generalization can lead to a lot of trouble and menace for the student.

3. Moving the goal post

The manipulators have every right to deny your goal and ambition. They call it the moving of goal post and this is how the public is able to induce bad and obscene mechanisms to it. The goal post is the ambition of every man to cater to the fundamentally obsessed question of the incident and with the passage of time, the manipulator tends to de-track you from the quest at the earliest. The track is therefore a sense of motivation for you and you do not get enough style of aspiration for the students and civilians. The idea is quite simple that the public is able to create more satisfaction for the public and with the passage of time, the manipulators induce havoc as well.

4. Changing the subject

The manipulator would do his best to change the subject. This aspect makes avoid accountability of his previous actions and with the passage of time, he learns the act of treachery and deception. Any time or anyplace, where he is not able to see the masterpiece of the subject, he tends to foil with the public and therefore, he is not even governing the matter of the public so that he could not even to the matter of appreciation.

Thus, changing the subject of any conversation is also a tool of manipulation that is required by all means necessary.

5. Name-calling

Name-calling is an art and tactic that can be used to induce marginalization in the incident and with the passage of time, it could lead to dilemmas and destruction. The name-calling starts with a mode of aspiration for the pupils but ends in utter destruction for the public. This concept can be easily seen in many areas and portions of the world and such a practice can induce horror and terror in the region. This practice of name-calling can be used in the factors that enable one with destruction and devastation.

6. Smear Campaigns

This campaign is used to address the horrendous use of psychology for the public. This is a play in which you are the victim and they are the martyr. According to them, you have displayed a sense of bad relationship to them and for that mere reason they have labeled you as a dead person. You no longer have a sense of reputation in the system and every time you encounter them, they tend to call you bad and the gone one. This aspect has many difficulties for you and ends up being a psychopath. This aspect has emotional issues for you, psychological issues for you, ovulational and many more. Therefore, smear campaigns are personally made to make you feel bad and obscene and with the passage of time, you feel very hectic.

7. Devaluation

This devaluation is not the currency devaluation but it is the human devaluation of yourself, you tend to be very bad and obsolete in your character that you embarrass every one's exes. You will as it is your pertinent duty to make the lives and ages of others feel embarrassing and with the passage of time, you control over your anger just to inflict punishment among the others. For instance, there was a time when people were able to cooperate with one another and could not try to defame others. However, with the burgeoning social media, people tend to decide the relationship of others by making them feel very degenerate. This is the crucial aspect of psychology, which could be very tumultuous for you and with the passage of time, he felt very bad and worse. Therefore, devaluation is meant to be an outlet of Body Language and it can be very harmful to anyone, who does it.

8. Aggressive Jokes

Aggressive Jokes are the modes to make others look small and in shambles. These jokes could be of anything like the jokes on individuality, the jokes on society and the jokes on caste. These jokes impose derogatory remarks on the individuals and with the passage of time, the individuals feel very bad about them. The idea is simply that psychology believes that manipulators could be the worst nightmares for innocent personalities. People can use the edifice of others to personally sabotage the concept of friendliness and equality among the people and with the passage of time, the people tend to showcase a system of defamation among others. Thus, aggressive jokes can be bad and hazardous to others.

9. Triangulation

This is the concept, in which the individuals tend to use the supposed threat of others to manipulate the innocents. Suppose there are three individuals in a room, two of them are having an argument about anything and the person sitting next to them is of a high caste. The manipulator would use the edifice of the supposed threat of the third person to deter that of a second person and with the passage of time, the concept of triangulation would be bolstered. Hence, the use of force and manipulation is done in order to make the third parties very bad and degenerate.

10. Use of tools

In this paragraph, the tools that can be used for manipulation will be discussed. These are sensory devices, visual sensors, automatic assembly, industrial manipulator and photoelectric detectors. These tools cast a shadow of degeneration among the personalities and with the passage of time, the people are able to have a list of traumata embedded in them. Therefore, with the passage of time the tools can be used for a stringent version of the collaboration.

Chapter 5 How to Analyze People

The final chapter will look into the thesis of how people are analyzed. The important contents of this chapter are as follows:

Secrets of Body Language

1. Body Language is universal in its nature

This claim asserts that Body Language is universal and needs to be implemented at a bigger level. No human being is immune to the dark conduct of life and he has to inflict pain on others just to exhibit a source of retaliation for the other individuals. Initially, he tends to be vindictive. However, with the process of time, he becomes more lenient and effective. But one thing cannot be ignored that Body Language is prevalent in modern and post-modern times and with the evolutionary crux of time, the human tends to be sadistic in its actions and gestures.

2. Body Languages the study of the human condition

Body Language is the study of the human condition and the condition does not necessarily have to be normal. The condition can be haunting and can be very managerial in its constructs as well. However, one thing needs to be understood carefully that the human condition has to be averse and adamant to evilness. This means that while studying dark psychology, one has to keep in mind that Body Language will inculcate a bad and worse human condition in them with the passage of time.

3. Body Language is replete of destructive behaviors

The Body Language has a concept of destruction that makes the human go beyond the character of positivity and purity. The individual is not able to have a stable concept of calmness and acceptability in it and have to be more lenient in order to understand the edifice of love. The individual faces some deep shrouds of destruction in him and this is the most devastating feature of Body Language in him. Therefore, this tenet needs to be comprehensively manifested for the proper extermination of bad feelings in an individual.

4. Body Language plants out a range of inhumanity

The Body Languages manifested in terms of inhumanity. The people that do inhuman acts are bound to construct in the name of dark psychology. The Body Language tells that people are the apex predators of the human nature and they can only evolve in the making, if they tend to be more delinquent in their constructs. This means that only that person can survive, who has the ability to rise against the odds and wants to be more compelling in its nature. Therefore, the term Body Language can also be described in the mode of inhumanity.

5. All people can be violent

The other tenet of Body language that every human, who breathes and has a predilection for doing anything will tend to be violent. This is the inherent quality of any individual and regardless of his and her intention, the individual needs to ascribe with the violent tendencies. Therefore, this tenet advocates that all people have to be very mature and strong when it comes to the acceptance of violent tendencies.

6. Body Language needs to be properly learned

This tenet of Body Language advocates that in order to know the harms and ills of dark psychology, one has to be incognizant of its progression. Body Language can start its journey as an effective wave of catastrophe and if not tackled with proper care then it can be very harmful to the people as well. In order to make a staggering impact on the halt of dark psychology, one has to eliminate any such mental or emotional prognosis that can lead to the emanation of darkness in oneself.

More in-depth techniques of reading people

1. Foot in the door

The foot in the door means that you are asking for a small favor first and then you ask for a dark favor. This is the favor that could be very effective for you and in term can lead to a bad and obscene prospect. The manipulator would first use the aspect of manipulation so that the people would listen to the manipulator and then the manipulator would charge his nutshells among the people. This is a devious terminology, which is designed to give more and more agitation to the public.

2. Door in the face

For this technique to b effectively implemented, it is important for the manipulator to ask something, which is quite easy and effective for you. The door in the face means that you ask for something very subtle and you tend to be affectionate in its manner. The asking is polite and it is something, which is easily accessible by the people, but with the passage of time, the offer gets more invitation and you tend to disagree with it. Therefore, this offer is a gateway for the manipulator to have his ends meet.

3. Anchoring

Anchoring helps you to give leverage on many problems and the manipulator can easily use it to display a sense of affection for the public. The affection starts with an offer and then the manipulator fulfills to price required to do the job. This pricing is a gateway for the personalities to understand the essence of anchoring and the people, get to know the essence of manipulation in an easier manner. This anchoring can also be interpreted as pricing and once the manipulator fulfills the ideologies of anchoring then the person gets the idea in an effective manner.

4. Commitment and Consistency

The commitment and consistency are a gateway for the manipulator to get to know the advancements of issues and with the passage of time, he also fulfills them. The commitment and consistency are necessary for the manipulator to the harbor and with the passage of time, the people are able to distill the level of trust with the manipulator. The manipulation is an important mode of affection for the people and thus, with the passage of time, the manipulator gets to know the advancements in a better manner.

5. Social Proof

This is a smart persuading technique, in which the person uses the social proof and it maintains a link of affection for the other people. The manipulator easily creates a sense of ideological confrontation for the people and the people can get a large sense of commitment through it. This means that there is a disembarking of an idea that is followed by all and by strong assertion, the person is able to have a strong moment of content for the people. Therefore, with the passage of time, the person is able to have strong social proof in the coming time.

6. Authority

For persuading anyone, it is vital that the manipulator holds authority in his hand. The use of force and the compelling nature of the manipulator will serve his interest in a better manner and together, the manipulator is able to cast a great shadow of maneuvering among the people. Thus, the authority rests in the house of officials and the manipulator and this technique can be used in many of the forms efficiently. Authority commands dignity.

7. Scarcity of Resources

Manipulators try to market their assertions in a common manner. They will show as something is unavailable in the market and will showcase its assertions in a common manner. With the passage of time, the scarcity is carefully ensured by the marketer of the individual and he is not able to formulate better postures of it. He shows as if he has the authority of all the commands but the scarcity of the resources is a way to dodge the loyalty of other personalities. Therefore, the scarcity of resources is a method to employ good means of manipulation for the students and the pupils as well. Therefore, it is essential to understand the nature of manipulation and regardless of any issues, the scarcity is an endeavor to boost manipulation among the manipulator.

8. Reciprocation

Reciprocation is a method to persuade as well. When times the individuals are able to harbor the context of reciprocation, they channel the crux of reciprocation. Many times, the individuals are not able to reciprocate the concept of affiliation and they want to unnecessarily reciprocate. This reciprocation is done to show how the people are able to transform their lives and they have the pertinence of other individuals as well. Many times, the individual has done something for the public and the public does not want any reciprocation but still there is reciprocation.

These were the techniques of dark persuasion and now the techniques of mind control will be

Case Studies and Proper Examples

1. Freud's interest in Young Woman

This was the experiment that was conducted on the behest of Freud's relations with young women. In his Dark continuum, Freud believed that women, who do excessive masturbation are designed to be bad in nature and this is an ill-coordinated exercise that needs to be stopped. His experiments were many young women and out of them, was a young lady named, Emma. Emma had problems with anxiety and depression and she used to do a lot of masturbation just to make the pain go away and ace the mental trauma. She decided that she will never ever dare to pursue a relationship and in order to ace herself, she went for a doctor, who happened to be Freud. Freud made her inhale serious nostril drugs, which made her go dizzy and how was she treated, remained a mystery for long. The concept of Mind of the dark can be seen in these experiments, where Freud is testing the enduring skills of Emma and wants to carry on the experiment at the cost of every result. The mind control process is clearly exhibited in this experiment and such kind of tendencies are easily put forward in the mind of other people.

2. Electroshock Therapy on Children

Dr. Lauretta Bender of the Creedmoor Hospital believed that children, who do not have any social order in their characters are prone to be tested under an electroshock machine. She would invite many students to her lab and would not see the problems of the children clearly rather would ask some tough questions that would draw children towards the confusion. When the children aren't able to answer it then she would put them under an electroshock computer and with the passage of time, the children would lose their subconsciousness and be paranoid. This aspect, according to Dr. Lauretta was a tool to make the children active and strong but, in its progression, the experiments proved their worth. Instead, piles of bodies of dead children became the terrible outcome of such results. This is the kind of therapy, where the person is able to have a strong version of its concepts practically and it can be put under the ambit of mind control effectively. The use of mind control can take the people to strong limelight and with the passage of time, there are many assertions and comprehensions in it.

3. Operation Midnight Climax

The CIA, in the mid-sixties, wanted to study the concept and outcomes of LSD on students and civilians. The idea was that the agency wanted a leveraging study on drug trafficking, sex trafficking and the conduct of sexual abuses in the city of Los Angeles and Washington. The agency would hire female prostitutes and they would send it would send the females to the rooms of drug lords. The prostitutes would contaminate the situations for the lords and gradually, compel them to spill the beans for drug trafficking. Here, Mind Control was passing with the concept of Controlling the Factor of Mind , where the agency, on the behest of its authority, wanted to have a command on the drug lords. Mind control of mind and personality is clearly put forward in this experiment, where people are able to have a strong version of a personality framework of it. The use of operation can lead to a strong process of cultivation in it and hence, with the passage of time, the midnight climax would lead to proper assertions in the person.

4. The Monster Study

This study was carried out by Dr. Wendell Johnson and Mary Tudor and they studied twenty-two children with imperfect care and zeal. They brought the children to their houses and created two groups of children. One group was given positive speech notes and they were praised for their slight bit of contribution while speaking. The other group was a negative speech note, where every word of the child, was belittled and defamed. The outcomes of this study were dark as well, because the children's mental cognition and behavioral practices never became as per the requirements of a sane individual and the research became very petrified about this. This Monster Study was never really published because of the fear that the researchers might get arrested for it. The mind control was the main pillar of this study and the people wanted to make good assertions in this regard to the public. This was done to make the process look all good and pale. Therefore, mind control is implemented in this experiment effectively.

5. Project MKUltra

From the year 1953 to 1973, the United States conducted a series of manipulating experiments for their citizens. The reason for such experiments was to induce, excessive drug use, the use of harsh words, emotional abuse, sexual abuse, psychological abuse and whatnot. The results became very hedonistic in their nature and ultimately the cases and subjects were meant to be shut down. The project MKUltra was halted by Congress and in time, it was politically removed for the betterment of society.

6. The Aversion Project

This historical dark process was a landmark in the Dark continuum. The apartheid era in South Africa was on its horizon and many people had to be displaced from their homelands seeking refugee in neighboring countries. The spree of homosexuality was prevalent in South Africa and they wanted to cure themselves in a therapist manner. Dr. Aubrey Levin was put in charge by the government of the USA to cure the plight of homosexuals. According to the doctor back then, the people of homosexuals were facing a mental disorder due to which, homosexuals were unable to cure themselves. They started fleeing themselves away and the doctor wanted to erase their sexual orientation by making them realize the harms of being a homosexual. The idea was that the homos must be displaced with nude pictures of gays and lesbians and they will be forced to curse them. Doing this, will make them unable to have any kind of love affiliation with any gay and they will feel all great and strong. Therefore, the aversion project was done on the sole purpose of how gays and lesbians are evil and bad in their utter character and quite possibly, this project can lead to success and sustenance. The use of Mind control is another demeanor of the humans and with the passage of time, there are many experimentations in the public through which the public is able to have a sound mode of mind control. The mind control is an experiment that can be used to make the humans and other frameworks look greater and assertion.

7. Unnecessary Sexual Reassignment

This process is a heinous work of mind control. In this experiment, the mind control of the public is directly controlled and the person is able to have a lasting impact on the people effectively. The effect of such a gesture will create more tendencies in the mind of the public and with the passage of time, the person has to be very cordial in its structure. Sexual Reassignment is a process, which tends to reassign and alter the sex of an individual through biological and scientific means. This process came to limelight when a nine-year-old boy's gender was reassigned as doctors were not sure of his apparent gender. His penis was circumcised during a mental process and with the passage of time, he had to be reassigned further. This trauma was a severe condition for the parents and they did not know what measures they need to adopt to finish this problem. They want to the doctors bashing their claims and the people had to face some observations regarding this matter as well. Therefore, this was a dark process, which was made to induce a horror spirit in the children of people so that they could remain isolation in their approach.

8. Stanford Prison Experiment

The idea is simple in its research. The research comes with time and longevity and this is This experiment was conducted in the midst of 1971, where prisoners and guard men were able to speak to one another and the people had to face the moral outcome of it. It is important to understand that the mind-controlling phenomenon of the prisoners and it is used to make the public go efficient about the mind game of the people. The idea was there needing to be the depiction of the cause between prisoners and guards and then their culture of interaction could be studied better. The people, who had been given the role of the guard were taking their respective genres in a bad manner. The prisoners began to enforce harsh measures on the guards and the guards were not able to confess the suitability of that as well. The prisoners accepted the abuses in a rational manner and the people had to flee away from the cause by all means necessary.

9. Milgram Experiment

Mind control was used to be done in order to make the conduct of the person more reliable and efficient in its making. This experiment was used to see the level of assessment of the public and with the process of time, it created more realms of study. This experiment was conducted to understand the nature of the Nazis, after world war two. This Milgram experiment was designed to see if the patient is able to see the harsh realities of life and can be conformed to the authority or not. There was a test tube that was placed on the sides of the patient and a questioning panel was placed in front of him. The panel asked some nefarious questions to him and made him realize that he was quite incompetent and could not able to answer good and subtle answers. This proved a dark mechanism in the minds of the people and the panel that psychology is very relevant in the scenario of people. Therefore, the Milgram experiment was a torturing way to express sorrow and sadness in the minds of people and hence, it was expunged off or halted by the people by all means necessary.

10. The Monkey Drug Trials

This event was an epitome of Mind Control in which animals were tested. They were injected with drugs and the outcomes of drugs were carefully examined by the public. The public rendered its advice to the people and made sure that how the reaction would lead the animals. This reaction was a necessary ingredient of the testing of animals and it was asserted in the means of people by all means necessary. The monkey trial gave a dark side of psychology to the public and with the passage of time, it was assured that monkeys are a detriment to society. Therefore, the monkey drug trials exhibited a darker version of the animals as well and people came to this result very quickly.

11. Facial Expressions Experiment

This experiment was conducted on the basis of studying the facial expression of people while providing them an external stimulus. In this experiment, it was asserted that people that have some mental troubling issues would be given an external stimulus so that the people are able to have an impact on it. The facial expressions are there to judge the internal conditions of the individuals and then the personalities of the individuals are carefully assessed. The system is quite inherent in this manner and the people are able to give proper justification to the external responses. The external responses include the use of drugs, porn movies, the inducing of drugs and devastation and many more. The facial expression experiment gives the students and the clients a justification that the people are not able to have a sustainable presence in them.

12. Little Albert

This was the dark hour of the psychological era. The founder of behaviorism, Mr. John Watson was deemed as the dark executor of this regime and he named some of the children to be equally liable in this regard. He would take a young child in his custody and he would test the abilities of him. Little baby Albert was exposed to many sounds and another stimulus, which made him feel quite bad and slurry. This was done to condition fear of little Albert and with the passage of time, Albert was made quite inhumane in this regard. Therefore, little Albert had to be taught something great about the channeling of darkness and atrocity in the present and with the passage of time, Mind Control made this landmark achievement that psychology can also be used to condition fear and badness.

Chapter 6 Types of mind control

Following are the three common type of Mind Control

Other modes of Mind Control

There are many other modes of Mind Control that need to be described as well in order to get a close look at the dark methods of psychology.

1. Dark Mindset

The Dark Mindset is a set of imaginary lines and circles through which the public is able to get a dark side of almost everything. These circles are based on thoughts, feelings and perceptions that can lead to the task of sadistic ion by a dark body. Once you are in this circle of violence, you are not able to feel purposeful or have any sort of ambition and aim in you. The psychological maneuvering of Mind Control can lead to the mental past of illusion and fragmentation that can be horrendous in their making.

2. Controlling the Factor of Mind

Controlling the Factor of Mind is an apparent real of possibilities and potentials that are provident in all forms of humans. Controlling the Factor of Mind will make you feel terrible at times when you are morally or socially dysfunctional. The Controlling the Factor of Mind can even welcome a spree of negativity upon you due to which you will feel ashamed and be in shambles. Controlling the Factor of Mind can cause a lot of tension and agitation for you as well. Therefore, Controlling the Factor of Mind is a dark emblem, which is stored in us and could lead all of us to horror and terror.

3. The mind of the dark

The Mind of the dark is a concept that will be related and comprehended in terms of

Astro-physics and astrology. The singularity is a small and dense particle of the dark hole, which is present in the center of the hole and it has a minimum space of energy in it. The Mind of the dark believes that people, who are inflicted by it are bound to suffer from the horrors of isolation and estrangement. There are at par with every condition of life and there is a considerable amount of distance in between them and the space that is coming to them.

Chapter 7 Mind control techniques

1. Gaslighting

This is the technique that is used to see if the person's words sound like his actions or not. The gaslighting is a method that can be used to question the belief of the personality and with the passage of time, the person has to understand the use of this tool to use the manipulation effectively. There is a set of questions among the public, used by the manipulator to dodge the essence of the questions and with the passage of time, the entire scenario of the public changes with time all because of the gas questions, asked by the manipulator.

2. Generalizations

The generalizations of a manipulator are a strong sense of demotivation for the public to withstand. The manipulator easily generalizes all the terms and tactics that are employed on a social, economic and political factor and with the passage of time, the generalizations come with time. The generalizations are important enough for a manipulator for the student to understand the essence of all compatible reasons for the public and with the passage of time, the manipulator is able to see the distance of the public go far away. Therefore, the distance of the public from the real cause actually defines the status of the manipulator and the manipulator can control a lot of sense through it. Therefore, the use of a generalizing matter creates more and more aspect for the students and civilians. Thus, the use of generalization gives impetus to the manipulator and with the passage of time, it can be more asserted in the coming. So, generalization can lead to a lot of trouble and menace for the student.

3. Moving the goal post

The manipulators have every right to deny your goal and ambition. They call it the moving of goal post and this is how the public is able to induce bad and obscene mechanisms to it. The goal post is the ambition of every man to cater to the fundamentally obsessed question of the incident and with the passage of time, the manipulator tends to de-track you from the quest at the earliest. The track is therefore a sense of motivation for you and you do not get enough style of aspiration for the students and civilians. The idea is quite simple that the public is able to create more satisfaction for the public and with the passage of time, the manipulators induce havoc as well.

4. Changing the subject

The manipulator would do his best to change the subject. This aspect makes avoid accountability of his previous actions and with the passage of time, he learns the act of treachery and deception. Any time or anyplace, where he is not able to see the masterpiece of the subject, he tends to foil with the public and therefore, he is not even governing the matter of the public so that he could not even to the matter of appreciation. Thus, changing the subject of any conversation is also a tool of manipulation that is required by all means necessary.

5. Name-calling

Name-calling is an art and tactic that can be used to induce marginalization in the incident and with the passage of time, it could lead to dilemmas and destruction. The name-calling starts with a mode of aspiration for the pupils but ends in utter destruction for the public. This concept can be easily seen in many areas and portions of the world and such a practice can induce horror and terror in the region. This practice of name-calling can be used in the factors that enable one with destruction and devastation.

6. Smear Campaigns

This campaign is used to address the horrendous use of psychology for the public.

This is a play in which you are the victim and they are the martyr. According to them, you have displayed a sense of bad relationship to them and for that mere reason they have labeled you as a dead person. You no longer have a sense of reputation in the system and every time you encounter them, they tend to call you bad and the gone one. This aspect has many difficulties for you and ends up being a psychopath. This aspect has emotional issues for you, psychological issues for you, ovulational and many more. Therefore, smear campaigns are personally made to make you feel bad and obscene and with the passage of time, you feel very hectic.

7. Devaluation

This devaluation is not the currency devaluation but it is the human devaluation of yourself, you tend to be very bad and obsolete in your character that you embarrass every one's exes. You will as it is your pertinent duty to make the lives and ages of others feel embarrassing and with the passage of time, you control over your anger just to inflict punishment among the others. For instance, there was a time when people were able to cooperate with one another and could not try to defame others. However, with the burgeoning social media, people tend to decide the relationship of others by making them feel very degenerate. This is the crucial aspect of psychology, which could be very tumultuous for you and with the passage of time, he felt very bad and worse. Therefore, devaluation is meant to be an outlet of Mind Control and it can be very harmful to anyone, who does it.

8. Aggressive Jokes

Aggressive Jokes are the modes to make others look small and in shambles. These jokes could be of anything like the jokes on individuality, the jokes on society and the jokes on caste. These jokes impose derogatory remarks on the individuals and with the passage of time, the individuals feel very bad about them. The idea is simply that psychology believes that manipulators could be the worst nightmares for innocent personalities. People can use the edifice of others to personally sabotage the concept of friendliness and equality among the people and with the passage of time, the people tend to showcase a system of defamation among others. Thus, aggressive jokes can be bad and hazardous to others.

9. Triangulation

This is the concept, in which the individuals tend to use the supposed threat of others to manipulate the innocents. Suppose there are three individuals in a room, two of them are having an argument about anything and the person sitting next to them is of a high caste. The manipulator would use the edifice of the supposed threat of the third person to deter that of a second person and with the passage of time, the concept of triangulation would be bolstered. Hence, the use of force and manipulation is done in order to make the third parties very bad and degenerate.

10. Use of tools

In this paragraph, the tools that can be used for manipulation will be discussed. These are sensory devices, visual sensors, automatic assembly, industrial manipulator and photoelectric detectors. These tools cast a shadow of degeneration among the personalities and with the passage of time, the people are able to have a list of traumata embedded in them. Therefore, with the passage of time the tools can be used for a stringent version of the collaboration.

Thus, these are some of the ways and tools of manipulation that can harbor bad deeds in the person.

Chapter 8 Use of neuro-linguistic programming to improve self-esteem, manage one's feelings and believe in oneself

Neuro-Linguistic Programming

The use of neuro-linguistic programming is a method, which is used to cater to depression and anxiety. On an international level, the use of NLP is done in order to make the programming look more easier and effective. Following are some of the principles of making the process look more effective and good.

Techniques involved in NLP

1. Internal Maps of the world

The psychologists try his best to make people aware of their potentials. The internal map technique is a way forward to make the people fully involved in their making. The internal mapping is the concept of all body parts of the humans and the people are made aware of the concepts of fruition and productivity in them. The internal map is a concept in which the people belonging to every aspect of the world are made more familiar to one another. The internal maps refer to all the body parts of the world, the language structure and the governing mechanism of the body. All these parts are interrelated and they are made more sound and sustainable in this regard. Therefore, it is important for people to make people make aware of the concepts involved in them.

2. Modeling

Modeling is a process in which the subject is told to model the behaviors, customs and languages of other people effectively. In this experiment, two models are made together in the concept and the people have to properly understand the structure holistically. The modeling comes with the passage of time and every behavior is carefully constructed so that the people are able to have a better understanding of the subjects. Therefore, modeling is a tool to induce more skeptic behaviouralism and with the passage of time, the people are able to come close to the mechanism effectively. Thus, modeling is an exercise, which can give proper illustrations with the passage of time.

3. Milton Model

Milton is a hyper-communication model, in which the person is able to have a computerized communication with Milton and Milton is a renowned psychologist as well. The psychologist helps to make the things in a proper manner and this Milton model will make you look effectively. The use of the Milton model will bring communication and character building of the individual and with the passage of time, the individual is able to make things more pragmatic in the coming. Thus, the Milton model makes the thing look more great and substantial in their matter.

4. Rapport

The rapport method is a type of method, which makes the belief of the personality look in a better manner. Rapport is the person, who has to be taken in the making of the individual and this is the process, which can make the individual look more dignified and designated. The ideas for this concept is very simple as it can provide good qualities to the individual.

Chapter 9 Who can be a victim of mind control?

The people that are prone to the following conditions can be under the emblem of Mind control

1. Plain Old bullying

If your partner or any individual in the relationship is trying to bully you then you are the manipulated. The result of the manipulation will come late but the present bullying is the result that will make you go restless and repugnant to conciliation. You will feel that your entire life is in devastation and with the passage of time, you will tend to be more and more exhaustive. Thus, the concept of plain old bullying will be a hallmark of affection for you and you will feel very agitated in its regard.

2. Home Court Advantage

In any manipulation, the victim can understand its victimhood if the person is playing his home-court advantage. This means that the person is not able to see the charms of life in a pleasant manner and he is feeling all bad and bodacious about it. The home-court advantage makes him go restless and in the passage of time, the manipulation gets stronger. Thus, the use of home-court advantage is a reflection of manipulation.

3. If you really cared about me

This technique grants a skeptic though to the manipulator that in order to make him more and more compulsive, he starts to ask more questions like if you had really cared about me and made me feel very great. If you had made me not so uncomfortable in the past and like how you can necessarily give more weight in this regard. The idea of this method is one has to be very relaxed in the confession and keeps on avoiding any such statements, which can make him more and more instrumental in this regard.

4. Emotionally Blackmail

The emotional blackmailing is an aspect, which will have a lot of confusions for you in the coming. It will make you feel more and more inspirational in the coming and hence, you will be able to have a sound connection of emotions with you. The emotional blackmailing, if it is present then it can make the wills look bad and in times, it can make a thing go in an effective manner. Therefore, the emotionally blackmailing is an aspect of manipulation and if it is prevalent in your relationship then you are being manipulated to a large extent.

5. Convenient Neediness

This neediness is the method, which is only done on convenience for the people. The manipulators will be using the convenient card to make the people be aware of the masses of the public and with respect to time, it is mandatory for the people to get to the affection in a certain manner. The convenience helps the manipulators to help the message of their utility go in a start manner. Therefore, if you want to have a convenient base of neediness in you then you can actually help others to achieve the best possible way possible.

6. Killing them with kindness

Kindness helps the individuals to know about the surface of the individuals. The manipulators use the edifice of kindness in a perpetual manner. The people will tend to look into the matter of others by possibly making them a culprit of their kindness and thus, the individuals can look into regarding in a possible manner. The manipulators would kill their relationships in a continuous way and hence, the people will come to know the edifice of kindness in a fair manner. Therefore, killing them with kindness will make the pupil know more and more about the just policies effectively. Hence, the killing aspect makes the kind gestures more productive and potential.

7. Very calm at the starting

The students tend to be very calm about the people all in the making. They make the individual more kind in their collection and the individuals make the aspect of kindness in a just manner. Therefore, the manipulators will be kind to you and if you want to make the best of the process. Try your best to make them manipulators go away.

Chapter 10 How to control people with your mind

The following tips can be used to control people.

1. He is charming and nice

The manipulator is all charm and nice at first. He would try his best in making you feel comfortable and gradually, he would impart his shrewdness. First, he would come in your comfort zone by wishing you birthdays, by giving you gifts and making you feel less agitated about anything then he would cast his dogmas. Once he knows that you will not bother him about anything then he would tell you to do anything by all means necessary. Sometimes, his manipulation is so strong and stringent that he can make you do anything even murder. Thus, this is the idea of manipulation that is started with charming voices and ending in catastrophe. Beware of such people.

2. Denial

The manipulator would always deny any assertion or statement of guilty on him. He would be felt exempt from any charges and would dare to see himself in the crux of any problem. If you somehow even manage to bring him in any disaster then he would just simply run away and would assert his innocence overcharges. He would think of himself as a strong mode of eccentricity and he would deny any kind of charges on him and would plead his innocence all over time. This is the true nature of denial that it tends to be very compulsive and bad in its progression and becomes haunting as well. Therefore, the denial is able to make the people look very bad and obsolete to the individual.

3. Lying

The people are able to lie a lot and those, who can actually conform themselves on it are lying. The lying edifice starts with the inculcation of hate speech and derogation and with the passage of time, the people tend to learn a lot of lying. The innocents are not able to see the manifestation of lying in their inner sides and they do not how exactly is the platform of lying quite degenerate about it. The lying helps the manipulator to learn more and more about the advances of the individual and with the passage of time, he comes one step closer tin dodging and abhorring you. This is the strong crux of lying that needs to be strengthened by all means necessary.

4. Excessive Flattery

This sign is of huge importance to the manipulator. The manipulator is able to do a lot of flattery for the individuals and with the passage of time, the individual can harbor flattery and sweetness among the individuals. The flattery helps to manipulate the individuals in a strong manner and this flattery can be of any side and sustenance. The idea exhibited here is quite strong as the people are able to create an environment of justice and order in the citizens and the flattery helps to regulate themselves in an effective manner.

5. Forced Teaming

The individual can use the teaming of the layers for his own motives. This teaming can be devious in its nature and can reflect many ills and whims of the societies. The teaming can also lead to social segregation in society and with the passage of time, the person can easily regulate its crux in a mature manner. The force teaming can appoint strong versions of impact for the students and with the passage of time, the individuals can come up with strong assertions. The forced teaming could be the use of any strength and value and it could be very destructive in its nature as well. Therefore, forced teaming is a sign of affection for the manipulator and it is destruction for the students as well.

6. Good First Impression

The manipulator will always do his best to make the best impression that he can in order to carefully influence the minds of other people. This is a well-managed task just to make sure that the audience is under the reflection of the manipulator and you will all mean necessary, follow under the trap of the manipulators. The good impression can be very expressive in its command and it can yield to proper potential as well but its lasting impacts are very pernicious. With the subtle use of a good impression, the person can easily establish his core links with you and can make you do almost everything. Therefore, a person having an expression of a good impression in him will be interpreted as a manipulator.

7. Pretending to be a victim

The manipulator is of a harsh and smart demeanor. He knows that if he will pretend to be a victim then all the people will listen to him and no matter what are the conditions his stance and statements will stand correct. He will understand this assertion in a jiffy and will do his best to make the public very bad and obscene. The idea is simply that the person is not able to convey his true propositions to the public and he pretends to be a victim. The concept of victimhood tarnishes his image and with the passage of time, he tends to deviate from the straight path. This mere concept completely obstructs the use of empathy from the manipulator's mind and with the passage of time, he feels very degenerative. Therefore, the person, who is a manipulator, will always have a sign of victimhood in him.

8. Silent Treatment

This sign is of strong admiration in the person, who is playing to be a manipulator. The manipulator will easily treat the level of punishment to the audience and while doing this, he will be silent and stringent as hell. This is the idea of concealing and secrecy that the manipulator employees and with the passage of time, he is able to impart a devious mechanism of dealing with thing upon the individual. Therefore, it is important to observe the silent treatment of things in the public and this silent treatment will actually make the person feel very atrocious. Therefore, in order to see the sign of manipulation the person has to be very silent and if he is found silent then yes, he is a manipulator.

9. Appearing to be selfless

The signs of selflessness are the signs that make the individual look very harsh and strong. The selflessness comes in the individuals either he has a golden heart or is he using the emblem of selflessness for himself. For instance, a boy, who is a manipulator falls in love with a person and asserts her to be selfless. In the moment, perhaps he is vouching for a love affair but in the true sense, he tends to be manipulative. He would cast the shadow of badness upon the girl just to have an advantage of her and even get something from her. Therefore, the use of selflessness is also a quality that needs to be strengthened properly.

10. Guilt Tripping

The idea of guilt-tripping is essential to understand as to decipher the nature of manipulation. In the guilt-tripping, the manipulator harbors the power of guilt in an individual and with the passage of time, he manipulates the other individual uses his guilt. He showcases that he is no the one, who is guilty and he trips the momentary aspects of guilt just to convey his innocence. This is a culture of guilt-tripping and it is easily found in all the corners of the world. Even international leaders use the edifice of guilt-tripping to transcend a culture of guilt-tripping. Therefore, it is important to understand that guilt-tripping can lead to a devastating blow of injuries and badness.

11. Shaming

When the manipulator easily acquires his motives, he starts shaming others. He feels that individual is of no worth and in order to destroy him completely, he must be shamed. He would shame you using harsh means, he would kill you possibly, he would employ derogatory remarks upon you and he would instill a culture of deviance among you. Therefore, the culture of shaming is found prevalent among the manipulators and if one has to recognize a manipulator, then he can use this edifice for good reasons. This is the revering identity of the individuals by all means necessary.

12. Intimidation

The person is able to intimidate the other personality if he is manipulative. The manipulation is a hectic task as it requires a lot of effort for the manipulator to intimidate you. This intimidation can be strong as it could lead to an effective mode of manipulation for the individuals. The intimidation starts with a turning point as it will create more efflux of opportunities for the personalities for you. This culture of intimidation is great as you can create more manipulative tactics for your self but in the end, it will be harsh for you. Therefore, it is mandatory to understand that intimidation is a recognizing aspect of a manipulator.

13. Diversion

Diversion refers to the diversity of opinion among the manipulators so that the people can easily lead to a better productive scenario of people to people contact. This diversity is important for you as it will yield a greater sense of affection for you and in the presence of time, you will be able to diversify your opinion based on a common strand of diversity. This means that the manipulator can use the edifice of diversity just to yield more manipulation and strength in him. This can be taken in the aspect of the plurality of opinion and in many ways, it can be dangerous as well.

INFLUENCE PEOPLE

Principles of ethical influence and secret techniques for: handling in people, being a good conversationalist, influencing corporate profits, influence on social media

FRIEDRICH LLOYD

Table of Contents

Introduction

This book will talk about the subject influence people. Influencing people is a social exercise, in which the culprit wants to be authoritative and manipulative in his manner. There is a beleaguered notion of evilness in disguise in the character and with shape shifting, gesture changing and dill dallying tactics, the person wants to claim leverage over the person. There are friends that tend to be influencers. There are teachers, who want to have a pertinent influence of certain things on their students and then there are leaders that want to influence their narrative at the expense of their political career on to the people. The influencing mechanism can of many intentions and ways but the most interesting and commonly conceded by the prolific intellects is that influencing is vindictive. It is for revenge. It is for maladministration and it is clandestinely and cleverly done in order to make the other look sabotaged. Therefore, influencing is all hawkish in its constructs and this book shall precisely deal in this study with full brevity.

The book will throw light on the topics like weapons of influence. What could be the formal and informal weapons, the strategic and malignant and many other weapons that could be termed in the ambit of influencing. Furthermore, it will characterize the thesis that why influence should be done for or against the people and how it is done? From appreciation to handling this book will give you certain limelight on the topic. What could be the business tips in influencing the people and how these terms can evolve in the time. To prove these assertions some of the valuable case studies from the past will be given to us.

Therefore, influencing people can be done in both positive and negative ways depending on the mode of construction by the other people and this book shall do his best in making the people understand why it needs to be done.

Weapons of Influence

Weapons of influence describe the thesis that how influence can be done in order to make other people look bad. The weapons could last any time and they can be very decisive in their construct in the coming time. The use of social media, the use of maneuverability and emblems of shadow can be related as one dimensional way of influencing other people.

Reciprocation

This is a reliable reciprocating tone in which the other member is reciprocated or complimented through values and gifts. For instance, a person is able to reciprocate a lot of persons through the use of soft language and this language can be done to manipulate also. This reciprocation starts with small flattery over certain matters and with the passage of time, the other person is able to come in the clout and ambit of the manipulator or influence. Therefore, reciprocation is an important tool of influence and it is used with respect to time and situation.

Commitment and Consistency

People, who are often in commitment and consistency, tend to excellent influencers. They believe that influencing is a token of appreciation and they are doing this just to imbue clemency in others. By clemency, they meant that they are fair and strong with the persons and the persons would resolve to them if they are able to be confined in shallow spaces. Often girlfriends that get aroused by many boys are able to get in their consistency and commitment of them and hence, their boys are able to influence them by all times and passes.

Social Proof

People who are able to give social proof of their care and adoration to others are masters of influencing. They believe that in order to make the proof more vacant and volatile, the constant flattery on social media is required so that the person is able to have strong components of love in him or her. For instance, a girl is at loggerheads with her boyfriend and the boy withers all the compliments on the timeline of his girl then sooner or later, the girl will burst in to happiness. This is actually a social proof that the boy is trying to give and all the doing persons, are able to do the same for others.

Liking

The more you like others. The more you are able to do influencing of them. Once you start to like someone that person comes in to your proximity. He begins to understand you and nourishes a complacent culture of affiliation with you that whatever you will say, he will abide by. The more you do this liking, the more you are able to have a context of love with him. In the initial sense, the liking factor will tend to deteriorate a little but once it is sustained and supplemented, it will tend to bulge.

Authority

Many writers of the current era believe that authority is mandatory to influence the people. According to them, authority comes with the notion of sabotage and influence and the person, who is authoritative wants his fair share in manipulating you. For instance, the teacher is the executive authority of the school and in order to make his ends meet, he is influencing people to make the decisions according to him.

Scarcity

When there is scarcity of love or authority, the person is able to feel more lenient and effective. The scarcity of love makes him more mobile to issues like anxiety and agony and with the passage of time, he feels more frustrated. The more aggressive and frustrated he feels in the coming time, the more he is able to rely on bad matters and hence, he comes under the influence of bad people easily. Therefore, the scarcity of love and adoration is a strong weapon of influence and the person would know its boundaries in the coming time.

Why influence is all about people, power and opportunity

This chapter will try to answer this question that how people, power and authority are the necessary components of influence. The influencing is done in order to have a strong social atmosphere. The influencing is important for a person to have a strong social and individualistic identity in the world. The influencing is made to make the people kowtow in front of you. Once you are able to do more influencing, you will have a strong set of mobility whether horizontal or vertical in the life and you will be able to garner more and more attention in the contemporary scenario.

It is also about power because the people that influence are pressingly powerful. The more power and agitation the person is able to get, the more he is under the ambit of influence. Influencing will involve strong tactical tendencies that can cater to the demand of power in the world. The examples contain of politician and diplomats that want to exhibit power and anarchy in the coming time. With the passage of time, the people that want to be more powerful exhibit a certain predilection towards influencing people because they want the use of influence for their own vested interests. They believe that power can manipulate people and can-do things in a pertinent manner.

When it comes to opportunity, the people who want to use the ambit of power must relate themselves with the use of influencing. In a mathematical expression, influence plus opportunity is equal to power. The more influential opportunities a person is able to get, the more he stands aloof of all other skirmishes that are happening in the status-quo. By power, the people of the world believe that the rising tide of opportunity can lead towards a strong influx of opportunity and power.

Therefore, these are reason that why influence is all about power and money.

What are the principles of ethical influence?

Following are the principle of ethical influence.

14. He is charming and nice

The manipulator is all charm and nice at first. He would try his best in making you feel comfortable and gradually, he would impart his shrewdness. First, he would come in your comfort zone by wishing you birthdays, by giving you gifts and making you feel less agitated about anything then he would cast his dogmas. Once he knows that you will not bother him about anything then he would tell you to do anything by all means necessary. Sometimes, his manipulation is so strong and stringent that he can make you do anything even a murder. Thus, this is the idea of manipulation that is started with charming voices and ending in catastrophe. Beware of such people.

15. Denial

The manipulator would always deny any assertion or statement of guilty on him. He would be felt exempt of any charges and would dare to see himself in the crux of any problem. If you somehow even manage to bring him in any disaster then he would just simply run away and would assert his innocence over charges. He would think of himself as a strong mode of eccentricity and he would deny any kind of charges on him and would plead his innocence all over time. This is the true nature of denial that it tends to be very compulsive and bad in its progression and becomes haunting as well. Therefore, the denial is able to make the people look very bad and obsolete to the individual.

16. Lying

The people are able to lie a lot and those, who can actually conform themselves on it are lying. The lying edifice starts with the inculcation of hate speech and derogation and with the passage of time, the people tend to learn a lot of lying. The innocents are not able to see the manifestation of lying in their inner sides and they do not how exactly is the platform of lying quite degenerate about it. The lying helps the manipulator to learn more and more about the advances of the individual and with the passage of time, he comes one step closer tin dodging and abhorring you. This is the strong crux of lying that needs to be strengthened by all means necessary.

17. Excessive Flattery

This sign is of huge importance with the manipulator. The manipulator is able to do a lot of flattery for the individuals and with the passage of time, the individual can harbor flattery and sweetness among the individuals. The flattery helps to manipulate the individuals in a strong manner and this flattery can be of any side and sustenance. The idea exhibited here is quite strong as the people are able to create an environment of justice and order in the citizens and the flattery helps to regulate themselves in an effective manner.

18. Forced Teaming

The individual can use the teaming of the layers for his own motives. This teaming can be devious in its nature and can reflect many ills and whims of the societies. The teaming can also lead to a social segregation in the society and with the passage of time, the person can easily regulate its crux in a mature manner. The force teaming can appoint strong versions of impact for the students and with the passage of time, the individuals can come up with strong assertions. The forced teaming could be the use of any strength and value and it could be very destructive in its nature as well. Therefore, forced teaming is a sign of affection for the manipulator and it is destruction for the students as well.

19. Good First Impression

The manipulator will always do his best in making the best impression that he can in order to carefully influence the minds of other people. This is a well-managed task just to make sure that the audience is under the reflection of the manipulator and you will all means necessary, follow under the trap of the manipulators. The good impression can be very expressive in its command and it can yield to proper potential as well but its lasting impacts are very pernicious. With the subtle use of good impression, the person can easily establish his core links with you and can make you do almost everything. Therefore, a person having an expression of good impression in him will be interpreted as a manipulator.

20. Pretending to be a victim

The manipulator is of a harsh and smart demeanor. He knows that of he will pretend to be a victim then all the persons will listen to him and no matter what are the conditions his stance and statements will stand correct. He will understand this assertion in a jiffy and will do his best in making the public very bad and obscene. The idea is simple that the person is not able to convey his true propositions to the public and he pretends to be a victim. The concept of victimhood tarnishes his image and with the passage of time, he tends to deviate from the straight path. This mere concept completely obstructs the use of empathy from the manipulator's mind and with the passage of time, he feels very degenerative. Therefore, the person, who is a manipulator, will always have sign of victimhood in him.

21. Silent Treatment

This sign is of strong admiration in the person, who is playing to be a manipulator. The manipulator will easily treat the level of punishment to the audience and while doing this, he will be silent and stringent as hell. This is the idea of concealing and secrecy that the manipulator employees and with the passage of time, he is able to impart a devious mechanism of dealing thing upon the individual. Therefore, it is important to observer the silent treatment of things in the public and this silent treatment will actually make the person feel very atrocious. Therefore, in order to see the sign of manipulation the person has to be very silent and if he is found silent then yes, he is a manipulator.

22. Appearing to be selfless

The signs of selflessness are the signs that make the individual look very harsh and strong. The selflessness comes in the individuals either he has a golden heart or is he using the emblem of selflessness for himself. For instance, a boy, who is a manipulator falls in love for a person and asserts her to be selfless. In the moment, perhaps he is vouching for a love affair but in true sense, he tends to be manipulative. He would cast the shadow of badness upon the girl just to have an advantage of her and even get something from her. Therefore, the use of selflessness is also a quality that needs to be strengthened properly.

23. Guilt Tripping

The idea of guilt tripping is essential to understand as to decipher the nature of manipulation. In the guilt tripping, the manipulator harbors the power of guilt in an individual and with the passage of time, he manipulates the other individual uses his guilt. He showcases that he is not the one, who is guilt and he trips the momentary aspects of guilt just to convey his innocence. This is a culture of guilt tripping and it is easily found in all the corners of the world. Even international leaders use the edifice of guilt tripping to transcend a culture of guilt tripping. Therefore, it is important to understand that guilt tripping can lead to a devastating blow of injuries and badness.

24. Shaming

When the manipulator easily acquires his motives, he starts shaming others. He feels that individual is of no worthy and in order to destroy him completely, he must be shamed. He would shame you using harsh means, he would kill you possibly, he would employ derogatory remarks upon you and he would instill a culture of deviance among you. Therefore, the culture of shaming is found prevalent among the manipulators and if one has to recognize a manipulator, then he can use this edifice for good reasons. This is the revering identity of the individuals by all means necessary.

25. Intimidation

The person is able to intimidate the other personality if he is manipulative. The manipulation is a hectic task as it requires a lot of effort for the manipulator to intimidate you. This intimidation can be strong as it could lead to an effective mode of manipulation for the individuals. The intimidation starts with a turning point as it will create more efflux of opportunities for the personalities for you. This culture of intimidation is great as you can create more manipulative tactics for yourself but in the end, it will be harsh for you. Therefore, it is mandatory to understand that intimidation is a recognizing aspect of a manipulator.

26. Diversion

Diversion refers to the diversity of opinion among the manipulators so that the people can easily lead to a better productive scenario of people to people contact. This diversity is important for you as it will yield greater sense of affection for you and in the presence of time, you will be able to diversify your opinion based on a common strand of diversity. This means that the manipulator can use the edifice of diversity just to yield more manipulation and strength in him. This can be taken in the aspect of plurality of opinion and in many ways, it can be dangerous as well.

Fundamental techniques in handling in people

This chapter will talk about the fundamental techniques that are used to handle the people in an affirmative manner.

1. Gaslighting

This is the technique that is used to see if the person's words sound like his actions or not. The gaslighting is a method that can be used to question the belief of the personality and with the passage of time, the person has to understand the use of this tool to use the manipulation effectively. There is a set of questions among the public, used by the manipulator to dodge the essence of the questions and with the passage of time, the entire scenario of the public changes with time all because of the gas questions, asked by the manipulator.

2. Generalizations

The generalizations of a manipulator are a strong sense of demotivation for the public to withstand. The manipulator easily generalizes all the terms and tactics that are employed on a social, economic and political factor and with the passage of time, the generalizations come with time. The generalizations are important enough for a manipulator for the student to understand the essence of all compatible reasons for the public and with the passage of time, the manipulator is able to see the distance of the public go far away. Therefore, the distance of the public from the real cause actually defines the status of the manipulator and with the manipulator can control a lot of sense through it. Therefore, the use of a generalizing matter creates more and more aspect for the students and civilians. Thus, the use of generalization gives impetus to the manipulator and with the passage of time, it can be more asserted in the coming. So, generalization can lead to a lot of trouble and menace for the student.

3. Moving the goal post

The manipulators have every right to deny your goal and ambition. They call it the moving of goal post and this is how the public is able induce bad and obscene mechanism to it. The goal post is the ambition of every man to cater to the fundamentally obsessed question of the incident and with the passage of time, the manipulator tends to de-track you from the quest at the earliest. The track is therefore a sense of motivation for you and you do not get enough style of aspiration for the students and civilians. The idea is quite simple that the public are able to create more satisfaction for the public and with the passage of time, the manipulators induce havoc as well.

4. Changing the subject

The manipulator would do his best in changing the subject. This aspect makes avoid accountability of his previous actions and with the passage of time, he learns the act of treachery and deception. Any time or anyplace, where he is not able to see the master piece of the subject, he tends to foil with the public and therefore, he is not even governing to the matter of the public so that he could not even to the matter of appreciation. Thus, changing the subject of any conversation is also a tool of manipulation that is required by all means necessary.

5. Name calling

Name calling is an art and tactic that can be used to induce marginalization in the incident and with the passage of time, it could lead to dilemmas and destruction. The name calling starts with a mode of aspiration for the pupils but ends in utter destruction for the public. This concept can be easily seen in many areas and portions of the world and such a practice can induce horror and terror in the region. This practice of name calling can be used in the factors that enable one with destruction and devastation.

6. Smear Campaigns

This campaign is used to address the horrendous use of psychology for the public. This is a play in which you are the victim and they are the martyr. According to them, you have displayed a sense of bad relationship to them and for that mere reason they have labeled you as a dead person. You no longer have a sense of reputation in the system and every time you encounter them, they tend to call you bad and the gone one. This aspect has many difficulties for you and end up being a psychopath. This aspect has emotional issues for you, psychological issues for you, ovulational and many more. Therefore, smear campaigns are personally made to make you feel bad and obscene and with the passage of time, you feel very hectic.

7. Devaluation

This devaluation is not the currency devaluation but it is the human devaluation of yourself, you tend to be very bad and obsolete in your character that you embarrass every one's exes. You will as it is your pertinent duty to make the lives and ages of others feel embarrassing and with the passage of time, you control over your anger just to inflict punishment among the others. For instance, there was a time when people were able to cooperate with one another and could not try to defame others. However, with the burgeoning social media, people tend to decide the relationship of others by making them feel very degenerate. This is the crucial aspect of psychology, which could be very tumultuous for you and with the passage of time, he felt very bad and worse. Therefore, devaluation is meant to be an outlet of Mind Control and it can be very harmful for anyone, who does it.

8. Aggressive Jokes

Aggressive Jokes are the modes to make others look small and in shambles. These jokes could be of anything like the jokes on individuality, the jokes on society and the jokes on caste. These jokes impose derogatory remarks on the individuals and with the passage of time, the individuals feel very bad about them. The idea is simple that the psychology believes that manipulators could be worst nightmares for innocent personalities. People can use the edifice of others to personally sabotage the concept of friendliness and equality among the persons and with the passage of time, the people tend to showcase a system of defamation among others. Thus, aggressive jokes can be bad and hazardous for others.

9. Triangulation

This is the concept, in which the individuals tend to use the supposed threat of others to manipulate the innocents. Suppose there are three individuals in a room, two of them are having an argument about anything and the person sitting next to them is of a high caste. The manipulator would use the edifice of supposed threat of the third person to deter that of a second person and with the passage of time, the concept of triangulation would be bolstered. Hence, the use of force and manipulation is done in order to make the third parties very bad and degenerate.

10. Use of tools

In this paragraph, the tools that can be used for manipulation will be discussed. These are sensory devices, visual sensor, automatic assembly, industrial manipulator and photoelectric detector. These tools cast a shadow of degeneration among the personalities and with the passage of time, the people are able to have list of traumata embedded in them. Therefore, with the passage of time the tools can be used for a stringent version of collaboration.

11. Do all the thinking

The manipulators will do their best in doing the thinking for you. They will think for you and will tell you the best for you. However, the doing revolves around the crux of manipulation. They are doing this so that you can be in their domain and thus, there mind control tactic is successful. This is the better prospect for you and once you do this, you are in the action of the mind control.

12. Starting an avalanche

The avalanche is a marketing firm that makes you strong and subtle in their regard. The creation of an avalanche is pertinent for you to understand and with the passage of time, there is a secret maneuvering for you and you will induce an avalanche for you. The avalanche for you is that you have to be in the claws of an avalanche for you. Therefore, the mindset of the individual is easily dodging and with the passage of time, he is able to have a control of the manipulator.

13. Ask for an inch take a mile

The asking for an inch and taking a mile is a concept that asserts ,the importance of taking things quickly. This means that the manipulator would cast a shadow quickly and with the passage of time, he would ask things for you which would have no actual reasons. This can be explained with an example. The manipulator would do a big favor for you and in return, you would love to comply him and with the passage of time, the manipulator would not take your compliments. He would ask of something great and then he would take a profuse amount. This is the basic tenant of manipulation that ask something else and get all-in return.

14. Always have real deadline

The real deadline means that the person has to realistically forecast a shadow line on you and you are not expected to do anything in return. The deadline means that you will do something for him and in return, he will give you proper isolation for you. Therefore, it is important to understand the nature of you and you will have the prospects in no time. The real deadline refers to the last concept of the material and with the passage of time, you will get a new result in the formation.

15. Giving ten times more

The manipulator will be able to leverage himself by giving you more and more things. If he does something for you and in return you do better for him. Then this is the mode of affection for him. Therefore, the giving of ten time will provide you a sustainable moment of affection for yourself. This is exactly the method of utilization for you and you will be able to have more relaxation of it.

Therefore, the giving of more things is actually a way to control the minds of the public and he will get more and more insight of it. Thus, the giving of more and more things will provide you with better affection.

16. Standing for something greater for you

The people are able to get in your mind control if they believe in you. In order for them to believe in you, you have to do something great for them. To an extent, that they will always recall of you while they are pursuing something and they are able to have a problem in any situation. In this way, they will harbor all the mechanisms for you that will induce a great sense of affection for you. Therefore, the standing for something is actually an act of affection for you and the people around.

17. Be shameless

The people are always shameless, who want to manipulate you carefully. They feel as it is their importance to have you on board for their progression. They believe that the people will understand you effectively if they are shameless. Being shameless does not mean that they dance in all nudity for you but in actual terms, they are able to have a strong sense of affection for you. Therefore, being shameless is an attribute to you so that you are able to have a precautionary sense of affection in you.

18. Eye seduction

In psychology, you can use the edifice of eye to eye connection in order to make the eyes look greater and more effective. The eye effect is important to seduce the other end of personalities. The personalities are able to have a great sense of seduction in them due to which the public is able to have fun and persuasion. The eye seduction is tantamount to give more and more value to the psychologists and in time, they are able to have more fun and zeal in the eye seduction. Thus, it is important to do eye seduction in the coming time.

19. Using the lack nesses

In dark psychology, you can use the lack nesses of other personalities so that you can have the leverage on other personalities. You will understand in time that the individuals will be able to have more and more zeal in them. The lack nesses can give you more aspect in their clout. The clout can be more incisive in their regard. The use of edifice can help you give more and more aspiration in the coming. The psychologist and the manipulator will use this prospect to gain leverage in the coming time.

20. Isolation

Isolation starts with the basics of brainwashing. The brainwashing is important to understand by the manipulator. The manipulator would use the edifice of isolation. The isolation is effective in its use and by all means necessary, the manipulator tends to isolate you from social order. He makes you understand that the world is not effective in its use and can be very haunting in its meaning. Therefore, isolation is a technique used to be understood effectively.

21. Attacks on self-esteem

While brainwashing, the manipulator uses the edifice of attacks on self-esteem. For him, the brain of you is of high importance. Whatever he thinks of you can be altered only if he wishes to change your brain. You will make the self-esteem of yourself and by the prospects you will understand that the manipulator is using this edifice to brainwash you.

22. Mental abuse

In order for the brain washing to work more effectively, the use of mental abuse is of high importance. The use of mental abuse will work in a practical manner and will thwart the conformity of the brain precisely. The mental abuse can be used of mentality and effectively and with the passage of time, you will understand that you are seeking to feel very obscene. Therefore, the crux of mental abuse will be effective for you in its making.

23. Physical abuse

The physical abuse will look into the brainwashing in a complete manner. Do your best in avoiding the physical abuse of the manipulators. Otherwise, you will find yourself in a turbulent manner. The physical abuse can lead to the tarnishing of the brain and you will feel very bad at the end. Therefore, the concept of physical abuse must never be allowed to be furnished at the first place.

24. Only allowing contact with selected members

Brainwashers or manipulators want you to contact with selected members. The selected members will cater to the brainwashing effectively and with the passage of time, they can be successful if you do not object them at the first place. The selected members will showcase a culture of degeneration among you and with the passage of time, you will feel very bad and bodacious. Therefore, the contact hearing is only important for you if you wish to understand the nature of the selected members.

25. Us versus them

This slogan will make you understand that the entire slogan of unity will forever haunt you. The brainwashing gets its momentum when it is trending at a larger scale and there is a policy of us contamination with the them syndrome. This means that the US is not able to engage the them processors and with the passage of time, the people are able to have a strong fan page about it.

26. Lie less and do more

The deceiving personality knows that he has to make sure of his conversations. If he lies more and more then he will get under the curve of badness and with the passage of time, he will feel himself to be bad. Also, there is a chance of him to get caught and could end himself in a bad manner. Therefore, in deception, the manipulator lies less and less and gets away from it.

27. Telling the truth in a misleading manner

Telling the truth in a misleading manner means that one has to be very effective in its regard. The telling of truth in a misleading manner showcases the strength of personalities and hence, the people are able to be maneuvered in a better way. Therefore, the deceiving personality uses the edifice of deception to make sure that the individual is all bad and worse in the frame.

28. The deceiver knows his target

The deceiver always does his best in knowing the target in an effective manner and when he approaches in an acute way, he tends to be very effective and efficacious in its rating. Therefore, the use of deception is a tool to know the target effectively and the time taken for its progress will also be used in a longer way.

29. Keep your facts straight

The keeping of facts straight makes you understand that what are the uses of fact measures. The idea is simple that the deceiving personality uses the facts straight and effective in its regard and with the passage of time, the facts are quite pertinent in its regard. Therefore, the keeping of facts means that the person is able to have a strong version of manipulation in him.

30. Staying Focused

The idea of staying focused is that the art of deception requires stealth and help. The stealth requires strong focus and assertion and with the passage of time, the man has to be very strong and sturdy in its manner. The focus paradigm will come in its manner and hence, the person is able to have a cure function of its people.

31. Watch your signals

The people are able to have a strong set of affection for themselves. The idea is simple that the deceiving personality will focus on the coming signals and with the passage of time, the personality will do its best in making the game more astute and effective. Therefore, the idea is simple for the psychologist and the manipulator to handle.

32. Always turn up the pressure

The turning up the pressure will always make the people look more and more agile. The pressure come with a stringent mode of affection and with the passage of time, the manipulator makes it look easier and more effective. Therefore, the use of pressure can ease the process in a curbing manner and thus, the deception will make the process more and more great.

33. Counter Attack

The personality uses the emblem of counter attack in order to make the deception effective. The menace used in this is that the deceiving personality uses the structure of counter attack and with the passage of time, there is a strong version of intellect for the people. The idea is simple and straight for the persons to come across and hence, the people are able to make more and more justice to this. The process starts with a better place to handle and therefore, the use of counter attack will make the things go way beyond the boundaries.

How to make People Appreciate you

Influencing can also be done in a positive trend. The influencing mechanism can be used to make the people appreciate you as well. Following are the respected techniques for that as well.

1. Always be Pursuant

If you want a boy and any one to be at your doorsteps then you have to be pursuant in all the matters possible. By being pursuant, it is important that you have to come close to everyone's heart, you have to be close to the aspirations of the individuals, must understand the needs and harbor the acts of others as well. You have to make sure that individuals are able to have a strong persuasion in her desires and you need all the prospects of pursuing an individual, in a dignified manner. Therefore, being pursuant means that you have to understand the significance of the individual's existence and with the passage of time, you have to be independent with her by all means necessary.

2. Be a gentleman

Being a gentleman, there is important rule while being a gentleman. You have to understand the qualities of others in order to be a king and with the passage of time, you have to harbor strong means effectively. The prospects of gentlemen mean that you must be able to give more and more credence to the value and must secure all the prospects in a complete manner. Thus, being a gentleman implies that you need to understand the qualities of noble man and listen to the others and people in a complete and compassionate manner.

3. Be complimentary

When it comes to handling, then you have to give all the respected compliments to them by all means necessary. You need to induce strong assertions in her that they believe in you and you two get along together. For instance, if they cook something for you then you must comply with her about the taste of food and better ambience. At any decision making, where they are giving her respective decisions, you must adore them and by all means necessary, you need to provide strong complementation to her by all means necessary.

4. Be creative

You need to be creative appreciating her and there should be not any issues whatsoever with her. You need to harbor creative appreciations as well for her. You need to induce a spirit of mobility for her and by all means, they will come close to your heart. Creation further bolsters love connectivity with other people and therefore, love has the ability to induce more creation in the love sphere. Therefore, in order to make the creation more worthwhile it is important to understand the love affair with an individual and hence creating comes with the passage of time.

5. Be intentional

The intention of a candidate is also judging in this regard and the husband has the discretion of the wife' love regime. The husband needs to be purely intentional in this regard and must have the ability to boost more love and adoration in the individual's heart. The ability to have the care for others is a sign of pure intent and hence, the intention of the man is carefully remembered in this regard as well.

6. Speak well of her in front of others

The husband needs to be well in front of others about his wife. In this way, the wife will be very motivated and the wife will be fall in strong love connection with the husband. The person will be able to have more connections with the person and with the passage of time, the husband and wife will have a strong mode of connection with other personalities effectively. However, if the person is not able to give proper concentration to the topic and is degrading the individuals in front of others then there will be serious setback for her. Therefore, in order to be well put with the others and people, you need to be very active and zeal with the personalities.

7. Be very protective

You need to be very protective of your wife if you want to be more sustainable with her. The only way for that is to value her with all the zeal and courage you have for her. You need to understand that how the love affair with your wife with vary with time and by doing this, you have to be totally comfortable in this regard and zeal. Therefore, it is important for you to make proper changes with your wife at any coming time and there needs to be no dilemmas and destructions with her by all means necessary. Thus, be very protective with her and have a strong love affair with purity and content.

8. Be a good listener

When you listen great you are able to have a strong relationship. Listening great makes you understand the inner voices of the individuals, in a much-contended manner. These voices resonate in your heart and brain and with the passage of time, there is a strong connection with the lady by all means necessary. Good listening also creates a strong sense of coalition with the partner and with the passage of time, you are able to have a lasting effect with the wife. Therefore, be a good listener if you want to live a happy and creative life.

9. Be romantic

If you want to have a long-lasting romantic event with your wife then try to appreciate little little things and feel pleasured about it. The little sayings of your wife when they are curling your hair, the strong rebukes when you do something bad and the bad repercussions for you if you tend to behave in a wrong manner. Therefore, it is important for you to boost romanticism in the culture of living with you wife and never be ashamed while romanticizing with your wife.

10. Just be yourself

The most important thing to put in mind while having an affair is that you need to be yourself with your wife. Do not try to be over dramatic and tend to induce horror and terror with your wife. Do not act like you are not the person you think you are and always be more compatible with the wife of others if you think you can suffice. Therefore, it is important for you to be yourself and never let the assertions float in a negative manner. Thus, the use of individualistic aspect will make you look more acceptable and accurate.

How to welcome every one and how to be a good conversationalist

This chapter will look in to this consideration that how you can be a good conversationalist and can a have positive side of influence as well.

For being a good conversationalist, you have to start being a good listener. In order to be a good listener, you have to come close to the hearts and minds of others and with the passage of time, you will realize that people are very clear and crystal to you. The more you come to the minds of the people, the more you are able to be a good conversationalist.

In order to welcome everyone, you need to be patient and be very pluralistic in the coming time. The more you come close to the level of proximity of others, the value you will get. So, in order to welcome others, you have to be a party man. You have to have a big heart and clear soul that can kill all the negativity around you. You have to understand that people around you can make a difference in your lives if you are able to make precise things coming in the time. Therefore, you need to be a strong conversationalist and a welcoming officer in the coming time.

How to win people to your way of thinking

This chapter will deal with the thesis that how to win people and convince them in a coherent manner as well.

1. Avoid contact with the manipulator

First and foremost, do your best in avoiding contact with the manipulator. This means that the manipulator has to be firm and fervent in this regard and you have to do your best in befriending them. You can also make the contact look very dismissal and there is no need for you to be socially devoid of them.

2. Say no to being manipulated

You must not come in trust with manipulation. If there is a friend of you that is trying his best to manipulate him and then you must say no and must try your best in making the assertions look very bad. So that the individuals are able to make the stand at a far distance and you are not able make an assertion.

3. Ignore the words would be

Often the manipulator uses the words would be. You need to avoid and must never the listener build the case on it. The idea is simple that do not build any such statements and assertions that could be harmful for you. Therefore, you must do your best in ignoring the words would be and never let any issue try to harm or dismantle you. Therefore, the ignorance is important for you to understand so that you can yield a good life.

4. Always set personal boundaries

Never allow the manipulator to be at your personal side. Always set some personal boundaries, which will make you look very bad and obscene. Try your best in setting the personal boundaries of the people and make yourself look smart and stringent. Thus, the idea of setting personal boundaries will make you feel very confident and compound.

5. Set goals and tell others to be away with them

The idea of setting goals will make you understand that you have a vision and an aim in life. The setting of goals will make the manipulator go away and he will not bother you no matter what. The idea starts with a potent moment of consideration and with the passage of time, it is important for you to refrain from any indulgence and incarceration. The setting of goals will help the manipulator to go away and the person will be able to have a lot of fun for himself.

6. Stay calm

Whenever you talk with a manipulator, you will notice that they will try to overcome your passion with respect to time. You have to stay calm and will be if you are able to create more strong versions of time. The idea of staying calm will make you fall apart from the manipulator and you will be at the epitome of your life with concentration.

7. Say no firmly

If there is a job from the manipulator and he tends to disarray you then you have to say no. No can be in words and in actions as well and can personally, make you feel very great. You will be able to leverage the personality maker and with the passage of time, you will see that the persons are able to have a sound knowledge of it as well. The manipulator, who is doing this thing will make you feel very robust and within times, you will get to know the aspects of it in a better way. So, say no to the individuals and with the passage of time, you will feel very great and effective.

8. Assert yourself and be hard

Assertion is a hard tactic for the manipulator to handle. The manipulation can be forsaken with anything and with the passage of time, the assertion can help you make more comfortable and relaxing in time. The assertion is a necessary thing as well and it can lead to a better personality as well. Therefore, the assertion needs to be commanded with full zeal and courage.

9. Practice self-care

Always practice self-care, no matter what happens. You will understand that what is momentarily required to dodge a manipulator. The practice of self-care will make you feel very bad and with the respect of time, you will tend to be very strong and stringent. The idea is simple that you have to be very cohesive in your regard. The assertion is simple that one can lead to the prosperity of the question in a better way. The practice of self-care would be effective. Therefore, it is essential for you to understand the importance of self-care with full zeal and honor.

10. How to get cooperation

You can get cooperation in the people, once you are able to make sound remarks about everything happening in the contemporary. For cooperation, you need to be very active in it happening and with the passage of time, you will be able to get more and more interests in the coming life. For getting cooperation, first you need is the ability to hard strong ways in life. The first you are able to get proof of the existence of the people and with the passage of time, you will get more compatible. Just be more patient, more productive, more reliable, be formal in your happening and never ever try to be more disruptive in the coming time.

11. How to win an argument

For winning an argument, you just have to listen the argument and try your best in making the things finer in the coming time. The inner happening of the side and the most callous things of all is to not do any kind of disturbance in the contemporary. Remember that the world is all about caring and adoration and with the passage of time, you will face the more virtue in you if you are able to make things all great. Therefore, in order to make an argument worth sounding, you have to be more complex in the status quo. So, be lenient to others and do not try to kill your soul while conversing.

How to change people without giving offence or arousing resentment

Using the following techniques, you will able to give less offence and depression to your persons in the coming time.

7. Repression

Repression means that you are about to forget the evil thoughts and mechanisms that could trigger agitation in you. You have to induce the spirit of repression in you so that you may able to forget all the bad thoughts and ideas that one has induced in you. You have to use the concept of acceptance and individualistic effort on you and therefore, you are able to have a stringent version of acceptance in you. Thus, repression acts as a strong defense mechanism and you are able to give viable justifications to it.

8. Projection

In this kind of a mental defense system, you have to project the positive feelings of any problem in front of you. You have to make sure that any negativity that comes in to your mind is easily removed and you are able to have a solid grip on your comfortability of the thoughts. You need to make sure that any such ingredients that tend to distort your inner feelings are not hampered and are not projected in your mind. Therefore, the very idea of projecting good feelings in the situations of bad feelings is named as projection. Thus, you need to govern these instruments effectively in the manner.

9. Displacement

Displacement means that you need to empower the inner thoughts of yourself in an effective manner and by any yardstick, you need to be pragmatic in the developments. The displacement helps you to engage others in a positive manner and you are able to have a sound impression of yourself. However, if you are not able to make a strong displacement of yourself then you are in the impression of the bad ones. Therefore, displacement helps you make the assertions come in an effective manner.

10. Rationalization

The rationalization mechanism works with the implementation of this principle that you need to come up with strong emotions in your brain. You can avoid any negativity in the atmosphere and most importantly, you cannot sustain without them either. You have to bolster rationalization in yourself so that you are able to have a sustainable feature of intellect in you. You need certain primaries in yourself while you are rationalizing. You have to be bold and independent in your saying and never let lose in front of others no matter what happens. Therefore, rationalization is a strong defense system that makes you believe in yourself and no matter where you go, you are able to have a strong system of catering emotions through it.

11. Reaction Formation

The reaction formation is a concept, which indicates that once the negativity has been uttered upon you, you are able to form a reaction on it. The reaction is that you do not need to have a strong reservation about it but you must have the credibility of conjunction in you. The easiest way for you to form a reaction formation is that you need to believe in the formation of strong reactions. You can do them anytime in the coming time and you do not have to feel submerged while doing so. Therefore, the formation of reaction creation is another way to make way for strong opponents coming in the time.

12. Denial

In order to make the emotional mechanism of yourself up to date, you need to deny any such restrictions upon you and must do your best in denying any sort of imposition upon your character. For instance, if someone is imposing any alleged mark on you then you have to make the substance of the world in a reactive manner and must not up bring the concepts of the loser in a bad way. Thus, the denying process is the process that cultivates emotional uprising in you and in order to make, the world a better place, you need to deny any such impositions on you.

13. Regression

This process means the minimum cultivation of negative process in you. You are able to dilute any such assertions in you that could lead to a catastrophe. You have to make or break the concept of affair in it and by the passage of time, you have to be very opportunistic in your desire. Thus, the process of regression is an important tool for you to make the negativity process go all away and you would be able to refurnish yourself in a primary matter.

14. Intellectualization

Intellectualization means that you need to provide an intellectual answer to all that chaos that could disrupt you badly. The intellectualization can come with strong potential making and can raise a bar for you for sure but you have to make it smart and interactive for yourself. The idea is simple and straight that in case of any negative emotions hampering you, you have to adjust your self effectively for the matter. Therefore, intellectualization comes with the evolutionary process and can be very binary for you in the coming time.

15. How to give orders in a good manner

The leaders need to harbor an intellectual model of leadership, where there are less disputes arising in them and there are minor conflicts in them. The very idea of giving an order is to make the people realize that they have many ways of commonality and with the passage of time, they are able to do a lot of things in a compatible manner. Therefore, for giving orders in a good manner, one has to be very lenient and steady in its approach. Leadership is described comprehensively in the following.

16. The Art of Leadership

Integral prosperity allows company to work in a creative manner. This manner is manifested if all the above mentioned five principles are made to manifestation without any hindrance or hurdle. The first and foremost component of this system is the art of leadership. Leadership is the ability of navigation that requires a lot of endurance and vision (Mathews and Katel, 2002) and verily, they are right. Leadership is a necessary tool in any endeavor and no matter what are functions and domains of the organization, leadership is mandatory to be implemented. It opens the door for justice. It incites motivation among the employees and makes them inspired to strive for more. It cannot be viewed with the same prism as viewed to management as both of them have different contextualization. Leadership is basically the art to govern the entire management system and management system is a minute component of it. Thus, integral prosperity can enable the company to construct a strong leadership environment and it allows the employees to company to perform and progress in good conditions.

17. Indicators of Leadership

There are many indicators or defining components of leadership. These include setting good examples, positive behavior towards employees, good salary initiatives and a creation of flexible working routines for the employees. Many researchers advocate these indicators to be specifically recognized by the company. (Jack Welch,2017), who is the previous CEO of General Electric tries to define leadership its term of setting good examples. He argues that a leader cannot be a manager and he need to refine the organizational climate, keeping in mind the working attitudes of his employees. He needs to come up with good examples in executing, planning and designing that could be exemplary for his career. Jack's famous dictum is "Do not manage lead", which means that leadership and management are slightly disparate from one another. In management, there are many stake holders like the construction managers, the subordinates, the project managers and many other stake holders that are less keen to impart leadership. They have compulsive attitudes that smother the workers and due to this reason, the workers leave the company for their own good reasons. Therefore, setting example is the first indicator of leadership and it is different from management.

Setting Good Example

The second indicator in line to setting good example is positive behavior towards employees. Kevin (2007) comprehends this indicator to be the important part of leadership. According to him, a leader is the one that sets example for others and in doing so, if he finds any opportunity in front of him then he seizes it. After doing so, he gives impetus to the practicality of this opportunity for his employees. For an instance, in Japanese construction industry, the Japanese mangers or senior staff take a lot of concern for their employees while their recruitment. For them, their employees are their children and they foster parental caring for their workers. They take the burden of their taxes, they provide company-based education to their worker's children and above all, they give flexible working hour to their clients. This is a perfect example of how leaders should come up with exemplary attitudes that could allow their organization to reach its acme and pinnacle. So, leadership can also be defined in terms of setting good examples by company elite brass for their workers.

Good Salary initiatives

Good salary incentives trigger a great working environment. In the twenty first century, everyone wants to have profuse money through which, the person may manifest his ambitions. If a company is able to provide bigger and better salary incentives then the working cloud becomes more strengthened and unique. (Ekinberry, 2007) points out this feature of leadership as essential as any other indicator. What happens is when leaders provide good salary incentives to the employees, there is a strong trust developed between them and the employees. Due to this trust, the leaders are able to observe strong tendencies to work among the employees and no matter where there want to deploy their employees, the employees will show dedication. Switzerland has a remarkable feature of this indicator. According to the statistics, given out by the major construction companies of Switzerland, the salaries packages for the employees increase on yearly increase and this increase in remarkable in its nature. The increase comes into action when there is a remarkable display of the performance, exhibited by the workers. This very idea has increased the turn out ratio of Switzerland in recent months and this policy is being supplemented by the policy-makers as well. So, good salary incentives on the basis of reliable performance also defines leadership and this practice needs to be established in any status quo.

Creation of Flexible working routines

Creation of flexible working routines is important to sustain the working environment of the company. There are many companies that have quantitative working environments but due to the obscene and arduous working schedule, the workers get frustrated and tend to leave the company at the earliest. This is bad and even on some occasions, it becomes worst. The notion needs to be changed and more pragmatic policies, which are inclined towards the whole-some betterment of the employees needs to be fostered. This is the indicator of leadership and according to (Richman, 2003) working hours reflect the apparent leadership of the company. Keeping in mind the significance of calm working hours, there is an interesting module apparent in the Japanese construction industry. This module is composed powerful naps, adjacent relaxed working hours, where pressure of work is equally divided among the employees. In this way, one can easily attain equitable amount of progress and according to (Volberda, 2014), equal relish as well. No one can infringe upon someone's work for the sake of repute or courage and no one is provided the proclivity to come up with harsh attitudes towards anyone. This process induces two things. At first, the employees proceed with calm and relaxed, which latter on brings upon good progress in their work. They are able to cope up with their aims or priorities and having a motivational leader at their back, they gain all the momentum to cater to challenges. Secondly, they are not afraid of failures or other discrepancies. They know that whatsoever is the outcome of their input, they will be examined through fair lens by their leaders and this provides them the necessary confidence to move ahead. Therefore, flexible working hours is an integral component of the leadership art and all those companies that display such an art are one step to closer to success.

Leadership theory

After discussing the various indicators of the leadership art, there needs to be more analysis of leadership theory. This theory, in its intrinsic sense, will give contextualization to the modes and norms utilized while manifesting leadership and it is pertinent for any nation to examine it with full brevity and honor. According to (Richman, 2006), leadership theory can be categorized in three principles. These are trait- based, situational and a behavioral approach.

The Trait Based Approach

The trait approach deals with all the important qualities a leader possesses. That could be the resonating spirit, an incisive vision, a display of heroic tendencies, ability to feel the pain. According to (Parry, 2012), who published an evaluative study of leadership, in his journal (Integrated approach to leadership qualities): Leadership traits are essential for a good management system. All these qualities amalgamate and form a trait that reflects a charismatic leader. Some of them are as follows:

Enterprising spirit

Enterprising spirit deals with the prime mixture of qualities that sculpt a leader. These could be the ability to harness pain for the weak and fragile, the tenacious mode of endurance, through which any problem can be catered and the hard effort, designed to nurture success in the company.

Loyalty

Without loyalty, there is no leadership. Leaders, who assume them as leaders, must endure mistakes and learn from them. They must be loyal to their workers or employees at all cost and never tend to misbehave or betray their leaders at any way. This indicator has special roots in management system as well. According to (Riecheled, 2013), loyalty is the backbone of any management system. This loyalty, in real terms, will bring about success and prosperity in an organization.

Leadership Motivation

Great leaders do not want to get lead or want to support a shoulder. Rather, they want to be in the frontline, facing all the odds against them. This is leadership motivation that incites a fire in their conscious. It compels them to fight against all the calamities their people are enduring and for the only sake of the people, they motivate themselves to reach the top position of the food chain. Thus, leadership motivation is essential to upbring the platform of Leadership norms in the society and according to (Hofste, G, 2015), leadership motivation bolsters productivity in any management system.

Integrity

How gentle and integral a person is, defines the quality of leadership in him. He needs to bolster integrity not only in himself but to his people so that he may see his message be implemented at all cost. This quality will create peace and order in the society with full esteem and make leaders more renowned.

Self Confidence

Leaders, who want to lead a nation, a company or an organization must have the quality of self-confidence. They must have this ability to endure horrific pain and after that, remain confident about their values. They must not mistrust the people for it will bring havoc in the society and must always be willing to learn from their defeats. This self-confidence is the key to their success and leaders must implement this quality at the earliest. French sociologist, (Benabo R. Tirole, 2008) defines self-confidence as a root basis for management system.

Knowledge

Leaders must always be open to knowledge and they must possess a profuse platform of knowledge in their brains. Knowledge cannot be limited to their personal or national history. Rather, they must know the slight of everything that is happening in front of them. They must know their public, they must know their regions and above all, they must come up with prudent policies that could unveil the coming happenings to them.

All these characteristics and traits form the trait approach and there are many other qualities in the leaders, which need to be manifested for communal interests. Thus, knowledge is eccentric in nature, which develops strong foundations for progress and according to (Popper, K.R, 2002), a knowledgeable leader can lead to more prosperity in the region.

Behavioral Approach

This approach deals with the qualities or doings of leaders that they actually do in their lifestyle and the specific habits, they employ to boost up their momentum. This approach can be broadly divided into three categories. The first category is task performance behavior, group maintenance behavior and participation in decision making.

Task performance

Task performance is the leader's effort to ensure the finality of all the assigned tasks of their employees. It is the duty of the leader to see if the assigned tasks are reaching their final timelines and if they are not, he has to come up with good methodologies and maneuvers to make the tasks go in right direction. Thus, task performance is the performance of a leader when he is monitoring the task of his employees and according to German political scientist (Locke, E.A,2015), the theory of task performance generates more comfortability in the leadership process.

Group Maintenance Behaviors

This is the attitude required by a leader to instigate harmony in group workings. What happens is that sometimes the groups are not able to cooperate or comply with one another and they end up in a conflict. The conflict becomes so aggravated that the group is not able to complete the task in a composed norm. According to (Gladstein, 2004), group maintenance behaviors are designed to create a stable managerial clout. Here, the essence of a leader is tested and if a leader is able to steer the command of the group to success then he is a leader.

Participation in Decision Making

When there is a decision-making process in front of a leader, whether he is leading a company or a nation, he participates. He incorporates is mind and heart in the decisions of the company and knows that it is important. It is important for him to incorporate his mind because his input will realistically bring forth the path to success for the company. He is the visionary leader, who has confronted many tasks in the past and through his norms, he can construct success for his company. Therefore, the participation of a leader in decision making process can enable the company progress and solace.

Situational Approaches to Leadership

Situational approaches are meant to distinguish leaders from others. In times of turmoil and trouble, leaders adopt a situational approach, which is based on decision making, orientation and motivational approaches. There are factors that affect this approach and these include: characteristics of followers, types of projects, organizational structures, personal preferences and upper level management's influencers. Leaders, who are actual leaders adjust their style of management in order to accommodate the different situations.

Thus, these different comprehensions discuss the leadership theory and this theory raises a question that is this theory applicable in all styles of leadership? The answer to the question may be yes but styles of leadership also differ from one another and there needs to be contextualization to them as well.

Styles of Leadership

When it comes to styles leadership then there are many styles to it. There is democratic form of leadership, where the boss or the leader is allowing participatory functions of the employees in the company. There is a laissez faire style, in which the leadership is allowed to manifest almost everything but more emphasis is given to finance. At last, there is autocratic style of leadership, in which force and compulsion is utilized by the leader to induce work progress. All these styles are apparent in the construction industry of the world and their specific contextualization as follows:

Democratic Style of Leadership

This is the style that argues for a participatory form of leadership. Leaders have to introduce freedom of expression, culture of critique and an atmosphere of tolerance. This way, the leaders are able to open their arms of brotherhood and compliance for their employees and can easily strengthen the organizational climate of their companies. In construction industry or project management, democratic leadership will be thorough input of leader in every stage of the project. Whether, it is planning, evaluating or execution of the project, leaders are advised to bolster strong democratic norms in the project that in return, may provide them the satisfaction of profit. Thus, democratic leadership deals holistically in building the crux of the organization.

Laisse Faire leadership

This is the leadership that advocates the sustenance of monetary funds in a project. In construction industry, the finance department of often industries has a pivotal role in controlling the total budget of the project. Sometimes, the leaders intervene in the necessary financial activities for their personal concerns. This is contrary to Laisse Faire leadership and in this leadership, the leader has no concerns about the monetary profits prevalent in the company and it allows the working of the budget, without any intervention or breach. (Marcus, 2008) gives incisive analysis on the formation of a laisse faire leadership. According to him, this leadership is exclusively important for the company's progress and flow provided the fact that the leaders will not infringe their roles upon the company.

Autocratic Leadership

Autocratic leadership tries to define leadership in a dictatorial way. Mostly, in the context of this leadership, the leader wants more of his concerns to be practiced. He has no concerns or attention towards the organization's role or progress. Rather, he specifically wants his values or endeavors to be forcibly implemented. Such a style is very impulsive and cultivates a culture of defiance among the working class. They become less interested in working for the clients or even for their bosses and want to simply quit. Once they quit, they do not want to be a part of their working brass and thus, autocratic leadership is harboring sardonic attitudes among the workers.

However, autocratic leadership has its benefits and potentials as well. There are some companies that do not comply thoroughly under a democratic leadership. They are just not admirable of democracy and they want some, who could dictate them towards success and prosperity. A similar case study can be discussed here in order to prove the thesis. American leading construction agency, (Pioneers,2009), in the year 2016 executed the project, which was the construction of a tall industrial building named fly towers, in the city of New York. After much discussion on its construction, it was concluded that the building had a staunch leadership style, which was autocratic in its nature. Speaking to New York Times, the then boss of the company, Mr., Henry

Osborn, stated that the leadership had to be compulsive as a mandatory tool to finish the project. According to him, the workers and junior staff were not prone to a democratic leadership, as they were mainly imported from foreign lands. It was, therefore, a compulsion of the leadership to be purely autocratic in its nature. Hence, autocratic leadership has both of its pros and cons and can be made to execution in everyplace.

Transformational Leadership

Transformational leadership is an inspirational and amazing way through which one leader can instigate work and progress among the individuals at the earliest (Avolio, 2004). This style of leadership has been mainly followed in many construction industries around the globe. Countries like United States, India,

Pakistan, United Kingdom and France adore this leadership and do their best in forming the seeds for transformational leadership. It has many prospects compare to its disadvantages. With the passage of time, the environment of the company challenges and there is an evolution in the domains of the work. Sometimes bigger and large projects, with a heavy scope arrive and the apparent leadership needs a minute change in its working. In such a time, transformational leadership plays a keen role as it helps the leader to transform his working brass for good and peaceful times. This phenomenon allows the leaders and working employees to stick to the plan and comply with one another. Transformation plays a key role in upbringing both the boss and employee in a beneficiary position and with the passage of time, it induces success in the projects. Furthermore, once transformational leadership is manifested in the contours of the projects it helps the leaders to reconcile their strategies with their employees. Occasionally, the leaders, in the pursuit of their goals, unintentionally, neglect the role of their employees and there is a serious void in the connection between boss and the employee. Transformational leadership helps to abridge that void and eventually, more trust followed by prosperity, is installed in projects. Therefore, transformational leadership is pertinent to the evolution of the project's pace and it paves path for the leaders and employees to bolster productivity in their projects.

Servant Leadership

Advancement in research regarding the essence of servant leadership will impact the organizational performance of a projects in a blissful manner (Stone et al 2004). Servant leadership is much more inclusive than democratic leadership and transformational leadership. It approaches to all those individuals, who are working at the bottom of the food chain and gives them a motivational impetus to strive for more. All those employees, who have been a victim of hatred, unjust polices and maleficent attributes, will, under a servant leadership resort to revolution and non-conformity. They would feel satisfied, when they will see a strong and charismatic leader, who has no vested interests of whatsoever and wants to install potential for all the employees of the organization. In this manner, productivity, hailing from every corner of the company, will come into practice and thus, prosperity will come out as a result. It is, thus, important to manifest or implement the credentials of servant leadership in every industry of the world to observe a magnificent amount of success.

Prominence of servant leadership has always been paramount. Researchers, scientists and even construction managers regard the servant leadership to be most important and apparent. Many academicians have regarded servant leadership to be the most significant style of leadership in terms of its working and function (Ethart, 2004). The words of servant leadership were for the very first time coined by Green leaf, in the year 1977. According to him, servants are leaders and they must never be exuberant or exaggerative about their styles and modes. They must understand that they hold the power of success and prosperity in their hands and by all means, they are the protectors of the society. Social order and control must be in their vision and they should not only anticipate them but try to practice them with full zeal. Only actions, coupled with motivational decisions, will be the harbinger of success in a company. Such actions must be employed by the leaders and they should never resort to tyranny or corruption.

There are two main constructs of servant leadership. One is the ethical behavior and the other is the concern for subordinates (Ethhart 2004). Ethical behavior is the attitude employed by the leader while he is leading or governing the organization. His ethics, his mode of conveyance, his attitude while facing failures and his moral compass, all together, form an ethical behavior that must be directed towards the success of the company. The leader must know his role and he should have a strong check and balance on his ethics. If his ethics are right, then his intentions are right and ultimately, he knows how to navigate the construction industry. Keeping in mind the importance of ethical behavior of leaders, the Japanese leaders are considered as role models. They have been idealized for their disciplined, fair and soft behavior towards their employees. A case study can be discussed for more easy comprehension. In the year 2004, the Japanese construction company, Shimizu Corporation, constructed a long-span bridge covering distance between two cities. Japanese Media claimed that the project was not being led according to his schedule and sooner or later, the project would be delayed. However, the ethical behavior of the senior staff inspired the working employees and within months, closed to its failure, the project turn out to be a successful one. This case study proves that if there is an ethical culture resonating in an organization then that organization can reach to its success in no time.

The second construct is the concern for the subordinates. This concern is equally important to the first one and under this construct, the leader, who is assumed to be a servant no must have a contended concern for his junior brass or subordinates. (Morales. ET 2008) defines this concern as a moral responsibility towards the subordinates by the leaders. According to him, if the leaders is not able to adopt a concern for his subordinates then he is not a servant to them but a demagogue. He needs to instill a courageous clout among the individuals that they must adhere to all the norms of Construction Company and while they do so, the leaders need to be polite and emphatic. Thus, the concern for the subordinates will eventually trigger a sense of understanding among the working brass and especially leaders will observe success in the latter.

Business tips to impact the bottom line

There are many ways to boost a business in a great manner. The first is the use of a strong management system, which can boost a performance of the enterprise. These are as follows.

Management Systems

The oxford dictionary defines management system as a working climate that impacts the functionality of the organization. In its true sense, management system caters to all the norm and values that, in a together fashion, govern the organization. It is a cluster of employees to boss relationship, the overall working environment and the important managerial ways that complete a project. (Ahmaad, 2018) contextualizes management system as the system that incorporates multi-functional activities in a project. By multi-functional, it is asserted that there are many activities that take place in an organization and they need a strong collaboration among them, which could make them united and composed. This collaboration is, in real terms, a management system and like leadership, it has indicators as well.

Indicators of Management systems

Indicators of Management systems are as follows:

Budget on training of employees

Budget is the annual or yearly related amount of money spent on employees or projects. How much budget is being incorporated to give impetus to the workers, how much money is being saved on employees, who wish to work for the betterment of the company and above all, how much money is developed on growth of the company. All these assertions comprise the annual budget of the company and in doing so, special emphasis is given to the training of the employees. This indicator has its pivotal importance and according to (Katel, 2005) the more budget on the employees, the more it is able to carve a successful project progress.

Relaxed Working Environments

Relaxed working environments normally mean the comfortable, the sound and substantial working environments that bolster productivity in the project. Usually, workers are not given relaxed working environments, they are compelled to do the work in acute manner and if they refrain from doing it, they are penalized for it. These environments will inculcate a strong napping routine, will give hygienic food without any extra calories, will provide extra holidays to relax and be pure. According to (Osvalder, A.L,2015), relaxed working environments are pertinent to create a potential working environment and many companies like the Japan and China enable such environments for their clients and it is for this reason that many productive and potential projects have been constructed in Japan and China. Thus, relaxed working environments amount to a productive management system.

Parental Caring

Many researchers believe that employees or workers are not given parental caring. It is true that the love and affection displayed by Parents stand unique in its feature, but if the companies are keen to provide parental caring to their employees then the results are very significant and profitable. Parental caring might include the discretion of an employee to take a holiday leave of any length or breadth, it could be the provision of tax payments by the employees and most importantly, it could be the free education for the employee's children. Such an affiliation is not new into the status quo. For years, the Japanese companies have been able to transcend such an atmosphere for their workers and the results have been marvelous. According to (Pole, R Waller, 2012), the enabling of parental caring helps to diffuse minor tensions in the company. They care for the child's education, they foster relaxed working platforms for their workers, enable them with extra credits for their hard efforts and provide them lucrative opportunities to strive for more.

Retirement Benefits

(Mathies, 2011) defines retirement benefits as those benefits that are inclined towards the betterment of the employees once they are expired or they quit their jobs. It sounds a little bit obsolete but they are companies that look into the safety and sustenance of the employees once they are no longer part of the company. This prospect helps the company to maintain its positive image among the employees. In this way, the company's image is not thwarted or transcended to conflict or difficulties. Therefore, retirement benefits are essential to create a recognized and respected image of the employees. Even, in the future, many clients get attracted to the company once they hear about the retirement benefits.

Brief contextualization of Management System

The management system is a system of management that is strategic in nature, open to the environment, cyclical in operation, striving for equilibrium and seeking optimization of all the activities in the project. This process, with its components, tends to prove all the cordial aspects of the management system and thus management system has an important role in defining the quality of the project. This strategy is designed to produce a product that is the outcome of multiplicity of people, process, technologies and materials that together perform a significant function. They contribute to a specific aim and therefore, produce a great market entity.

In order of the management system to proceed, it is pertinent that the system may proceed in a positive direction. There are some elements that steer the management system in a positive direction. This include the benchmarking of the organizations, analysis and decision making, output of the system and employee satisfaction. Following is the necessary detail of all the above-mentioned elements.

Benchmarking of an organization.

When benchmarking of an organization is done, the very idea lies in learning from an organization. The organization that is learning and wants to implement successful initiatives for its progress is under an aim to seek guidance from its bench mark organization. The bench mark organization could be any organization belonging to various domains. The first and foremost reason behind this initiative is that the organization wants to manifest its objectives and anticipates its success while doing this. Every now and then, new technology is being introduced and the construction industry is changing. Companies want to share knowledge, share technology that in latter, could be productive enough for their prosperous future. According to (Borgan, 2004), benchmarking of an organization helps to define the proper constructs of an organization. Thus, benchmarking an organization can be helpful in the future for both the learning and giving organization.

Analysis and Decision Making

Analysis and Decision Making is the important role, which is implemented by the manager or the leader of the management system. It involves the apt decision-making policy or process through which the management system is able to incorporate the total progress of the project. Various stages of the project like the designing, the evaluation and the execution are concrete phases of a project cycle and they require diligent attention. Any management system that is able to provide successive initiatives to analysis and decision making of any phase of the project is said to be in coherence with success. According to (Janis, I.L, 2017), the prospects of analysis and decision-making help to create a strenuous management system. This data systematically introduces positive norms in the project and make the project one step closer to prosperity. Thus, in total, there is an organizational improvement in the project's pace regarding its path and there must be a strong emphasis to analysis and decision-making portion.

Customer Focused Improvements

(Bergman, 2010) defines management system in terms of customer improvements. Customer focused improvements help to create a strong definition of a management system by inculcating a trust bound between the company and the customer. These improvements are intended to help the customer in achieving the highest level of comfort and profit. They include the revision of drawings, understanding the customer requirements, carefully listening to the feedback of the customers, employing a warm attitude among the customers and catering to their every demand with full honor and zeal.

Through this mechanism, the business or any enterprise will grow to pinnacle and setting a strong example of personal love and freedom to the working brass, there would be a lot to learn in the coming by the business men.

How influence people are used in social media

The case study of universities

This case study throws a light on the thesis that how the use of social media is very impact full in the contemporary.

The edifice of social media is burgeoning in the contemporary. Many customers, clients and Facebook users are trending their social lives, in their unique and effective manner. Universities or colleges have students that want to averse their lives on social media profiles. This description will briefly look into the modes and methods of social media users. The college selected for the examination is Brooklyn college and its respective Facebook and twitter pages will be brought to study. A comparison will also be generated among

Brooklyn college, Yale University, Columbia, and CUNY university to understand the nature of posting, efficiency of socialization done by students, teachers and other faculty members, and lastly, the material being posted on social platforms.

Starting with Columbia University, it has an efficient and integrating Facebook page, where it channelizes social events, alumni reunions, cultural talks, entertaining features like the movie featuring of a novel, written by a Columbian Alumni, reflecting international days with zeal, showcasing affiliation among individuals and some important scientific laurels. Each and every notion needs some contextualization. Social events, create a euphoric sense of togetherness among the Columbians and there are bachelor parties, farewells, assimilating dinners and what not. All are posted vigorously on the page and the students can even contribute on these pages with some funny and sarcastic assertions.

Alumni reunions are the reunions of old and passed students, who are the at the phase of job or any practical doing. They will come after a long time and have a contended time, where they will recall all their pleasant memories and engage in exhilarating conversations regarding time, politics and society. Pictures, videos and every emphasis will be on the page and the students will feel enamored while seeing these happenings on the page. There will be some blogs or articles asserting the presence of a nearby international day like the international day of peace, environment, book, water and Earth. Many marriage proposals are depicted on the page, which is then enthusiastically welcomed by the Columbian polity. There are even tertiary engagements that are visualized on the page and such an action boosts harmony and affection among the individuals. Certain theatre depictions followed with engineering and scientific laurels are also presented on the page with embellished details of a Columbian literary figure. Thus, social media usage on Columbia is paramount to endure unity and relish among the students.

When it comes to posting by whom and their followings, there is a profuse network of Columbian and non-Columbian students that are following all these leads with full zeal and sincerity. Followers range in the number of thousands and more connectors are being observed in the contemporary.

Next in the description, comes the prestigious institute of Yale university, which has an enriched history of producing literary, scientific and research iconoclasts. The university specializes in many fields and features economics, business administration, engineering and social subjects. Its page, like wise Columbian University, is emphatic to many social media usages. Basic and important posts on the page are: alumni reunions, historical tributes to revered political events, laudable inventions by Yale students or faculty members, harmonious gatherings and commemoration of many cultural events. All these postings are admired by the students and they provide their affectionate responses with full zeal and courage. Faculty members share their posting aspirations and their admirations are ubiquitous. This means they want to distill the moments of courage and study everywhere. Thus, Yale university is fostering an engaged level of social media usage on its social pages and it is quite appreciable.

When it comes to Brooklyn college, there is a collage of pluralistic students, who are from various ethnic backgrounds and the university's Facebook page also promote multiplicity of culture, accommodation of values and amalgamation of various norms with shear nobility. On the Facebook page of Brooklyn college, one can find exquisite blogging of nature, scientific tools and inventions, reflections upon daily news and events by notable personalities, graduated from Brooklyn College. Also, there is a collage of cultural events, societal gatherings and political conversations, which are enthusiastically posted by students on the page. The faculty members share their pride while commenting and acknowledging the promotion of major events on the social page. While comparing Brooklyn to City University of New York (CUNY), the university has a different clout of social posting on its page. It contains more of political news happening in the status quo, it reflects upon social notions like the awareness campaigns regarding health, social order and social prosperity. Also, there are some notable recognitions of work relating sci-fiction, practiced by the university's alumni. There are some fellows ship programs that provide educational progress to students and there are some proficient policies, devised by the administration of the University to give moral and sound knowledge about daily happenings.

The respondents on the page of CUNY are also very vibrant in their nature and they also tend to be the zeitgeist of all the issues happening around them. Thus, the page of Brooklyn change provides a wave of knowledge, entertainment and relish for its students, faculty members and respected authorities and as compared to CUNY, it gives more ingenuity to the issues.

The Brooklyn college is using the Facebook Page and the Twitter page in the best possible way, Best, because, the students are gaining knowledge, they are in cognizant of daily happenings, there is a clout of integrated societies that are profusely active on the page, the pages are providing a breathing relish to the students and there are many entertaining features, available on the page. Most surprisingly, there are also rhapsodic teachers, who want to show their passion for the betterment and up-bringing of the students, available on the student. Therefore, in a crystal-clear manner, the pages of Brooklyn college are ameliorating the mental and personal developments of the students. In terms of recommendations, there are many loopholes in the social flux of Brooklyn college and they can be improved while catering to these recommendations.

First and foremost, all students need to be encouraged to channelize their esteemed contribution in socialization on the page. No ethnical or racial segregation needs to be developed at the moment and all must be aware of the surroundings. Furthermore, on the page, there should be polls or referendums or asking questions about the betterment of the social fabric and all the proponents of the page should be encouraged to do so. In this way, with the prospects of social improvisation, the pages could develop more enriched content on its surface. Last but not the least, the admins of the pages need to come up with qualitative content on the page, in subjects of study, higher education, economics, politics and society. Thus, with these recommendations, the Brooklyn college can advance their social associations with anyone and can give prospects in all aspects

The Hunter college of CUNY is of stringent importance, as on its page, one can see the presence of theatrical depictions, practiced by students. The college specializes in art, music, poetry and dance, in a more enthusiastic manner as compare to the afore mentioned colleges and universities. The students and teachers often come and address important issues on the page and there is a remarkable presence of thirty thousand and more people on it. The responses on the social media pages of Hunter are more done by outsiders, as it many vouch to be a part of this institution. Many fellowship programs, including the Jeannett K. Watson, full bright scholarships and various cultural events for various ethnicities are conducted and promoted using the page of Hunter college. Therefore, the Hunter college is famous for giving literary impetus to its followers on its page.

Name of the University	Message in the Posting	Who is posting	Schedule of Posting	Followers and Responses
Columbia University	Universalization of education, music festivals and alumni reunions	University Administration only	Monthly basis	Students, outsiders and Faculty members respond. Followers are in the range of 3 to 4 million.
Brooklyn College	More Emphasis to Societal grooming and blogging about self-grooming	University Staff and students	Weekly Basis	Students respond and followers lie within the range of 37 thousand to 38 thousand
Yale University	Historical importance and up bringing the morale of students through education and strive for knowledge	ALL	Daily Basis	All the faculty members respond enthusiastically and the followers lie in the range of 1.3 Million
Hunter College of CUNY	Literary depiction of Art and Acting	Students and College's administration	Daily Basis and Monthly Basis	Students, faculty members and Administration. Range is in the value of 34k.

In a nutshell, social media usages among the Universities are of potent importance. Whether it is Yale, Brooklyn College, Harvard or even Columbian University, there is a rising tide of learning apparent on its pages. The response factor of all of these universities is variant in its nature and will keep on effecting the minds of the public with full content.

Business case studies in influence

The business case studies will tell the reader that how eminent intellectuals were able to boost their business in the coming time.

What business case studies of Steve jobs, Starbucks and other marketing firms had in common.

They did the following with full zeal and courage.

Research and qualitative research

Every venture and any mission need some proper delving of it. One has to be in cognizant of all the proper requirements that can initiate a business in the first place. In the initiation, one could be the starting steps that can yield better results of a startup and what things are needed to be avoided? What kind of an entrepreneurial strategy could come in handy and what will be the components of such a strategy? All those questions need to be answered in full brevity and any hurdle or confusion regarding the progress of the business must be necessarily eliminated.

By an entrepreneurial strategy, one can relate the definition of value chain strategy, intellectual property strategy and value capture strategy. All these strategies require a miniscule level of contextualization for better comprehension. Value chain strategy deals with the fact that the business overall run will be collaborative in its nature. There will be more research in its constructs and all those, members, whether a part of a supply chain or not will be given equal amount of work impetus. Their ideas will be adored and with evolving business plans, they will be used to up bring the level of productivity to its pinnacle. For this mindset of business, a research model is required that is complimentary for both the users and the clients. Thus, the value chain model, if applied, needs a proper researching mechanism and it is collaborative in its nature.

The intellectual property strategy is a strategy that revolves around cooperative competition. This is the competition that needs to be understood first and likewise value chain, one has to research as well in it. The competition means that the company will compete with other potentially strong bidders of food chain or other business ventures but will cooperate with its own chains and franchises. This asserts that if pizza hut is launching its franchise then it will cooperate with other franchises of pizza hut in the area. However, it will do robust competition, in terms of client capture, proper functioning of the products and good reflection of its name, with the other companies that do not fall in its category. So, this business strategy also involves comprehensive researching and with its competitiveness, it tends to cast a realistic business module for the businessmen.

The last but not the least is the value capture, which has an epicenter of competition. There is no competition in it. There is no selective cooperation and absolute cooperation in it and one is digging the rabbit hole for one's whole means. This means that the researching, one will be doing will be done for oneself and there will be no sharing in this regard. So, this model bolsters realistic competition and with strong research engine, this strategy personifies the business theme.

In the above-mentioned strategies, one thing is common, which is researching. One has to research if one wants mental solace, professional equilibrium and personal motivation.

What is the purpose of the plan?

Business can be done for many purposes. It can be done to attain a strong and vast surplus amount of money. It can be done to acquire personal motives that could be vindictive or very caring in its nature. Also, simply, it can be done to meet the ends of a living and there are many more reasons attached to it. So, if one is starting a business then one must carefully know the purpose of the business plan. It is sometimes ok to get confused about the business model and its purpose but the more one gets conformed with the actual notions, the more one is able to attain purity and productivity. Because without a business plan, there is no proper lead to a business. There is no proper direction and definitely, no direction. So, in order to qualify for strong state of affairs in a business regime, one needs to holistically construct the essentialities of a business model and with the passage of time, it could lead to a strong result. Therefore, it is mandatory to have a purpose of the business regime, in the mind and then one can start the business with clear insight.

Creating a strong company profile

The era of social media and vibrant media outlets does not allow individuals to hide behind excuses and come with simple company profiling. No one is arguing for exuberance or exaggeration of the company profile but it must have a clear-sighted, crystal clear and a callous company name, scope and objectives that could hit the bull's eye for the audience. The vision should be so perfect that even a layman can relate to the cause of the business profile and might possibly, be a member of it. There is no need to create aesthetic graphics around the profile and use flowery language to describe but while presenting, one has to be simple and succinct. For instance, one is launching a clothing franchise, with a slogan, comfort with cooperation. This means that for more procurement of the shirts, one has to be given concessions and the more concessions, given by the company, the more shirts one will buy.

This slogan is easy to comprehend and any minute IQ guy will clearly get it.

However, the problem comes when excessive market exaggeration comes to play and the art of clear marketing goes to shambles. Like this same slogan can got to wrong interpretations, if it becomes like get your efficient t shirt within the reach of two hours or something that makes the slogan sound more melodramatic. This is not right and one has to clear strong visions that could highlight the message of the slogan in simple ways.

Also, the man power that can become very efficient in its making, should be considered comprehensively while creating a strong business profile. The men that lead your business must be capacitated with leadership, tenacity, creativity, maturity, plurality of thoughts and productive mindsets that could be harnessed in any amount of time. Only then the business will transcend to heights of success and within no time, one can be clear-sighted with its approach and attain all the maxims of excellence.

Documentation of all aspects of business

There needs to be the documentation of all the aggressive market pillars that reflect the pertinence of the business. This documentation is the clear writing and consideration of introduction of new products, extension of market territories, the boost of sales with the passage of time, the entering into long contracts of the business players, the refining of a product, and the enhancement of marketing engines. All these aspects need to be clearly guided and appreciated before the creation of a startup. The introduction of new products means that every product, whether of cosmetics or clothing, needs to be properly branded. There must be a generic version of its branding and the product must be equally distributed among the exhibitors. In case of extension of market territories, all those market firms that have an entrepreneurial linkage with the business must be brought into collaboration and any piece of advice that could be effective for the learning of the business must be catered properly. The boost of sales means that the sales schedule must be thoroughly incorporated in the business regime and with the passage of time, a strong version of boost sales must be proportioned properly. In this way, the documentation is constructed properly and the people are able to get their startups reach the acme of prosperity in no time.

Know your audience and make the business adaptable

For any start up to come across with the possibility of a progress, a clear-sighted audience needs to be defined. This audience can be defined by distributing a survey-based questionnaire among the people and after careful assessment of the questionnaire, incisive deductions can be drawn. These deductions must cater to the regard of the nature of the start up and the whims and fancies of the business. Also, knowing the possibility that either the business is able to engage with the audience or not? And what can be done in order to make it more lenient with the business style. These aspects are worthy to be discussed and implemented with the strong version of motivation and thus, the audience will help to construct a business plan or module in no time.

Explanation of caring

Caring is the proper soul for business. If one is not in love with the business then surely, one has to suffer devastating repercussions. Being in love means that no matter what are the odds, the ship of business engine has to sail through thick and thin and no excuses are to be tolerated while deciding the plan of the business. Also, the reflection of a pertinent content coupled by a skilled horsepower of human can also give impetus to the importance of caring. When one will care, the people that are the spectators of the business, will be more attracted to the business and they will join the lead of the business in no time. Moreover, any foes that are ought to be revealed in the past will be carefully constructed and with the passage of time, the business plan will be properly constructed and implemented.

Conducting a personal evaluation

If one wants to be the connoisseur of a business then personal evaluation is must. Personal evaluation means the thorough assessment of one's conscience and plan making due to which one can relate oneself to the business. What are the wrong doings of the business? How to make them correct and what particular strategies are required for this task? All these are carefully examined and answered, on a personal level, when one is conducting a personal evaluation. Any issues that tend to overwhelm the person's motives are expunged through a strong though personal process. Also, through consultancy, any modes of negativity are precisely removed and with the passage of time any act of hurdle is carefully examined and it is removed with the passage of time. Therefore, the conduction of a personal evaluation is deemed necessary in order to have a business plan carefully constructed.

Start the planning process

The planning process will be initiated once the business strategies that have been defined earlier are carefully implemented. On this process, you can easily start the planning process and with time, you can execute all the fundamentals to it with all the possible urge and patience. This planning process will have certain paper work and some affiliation with the law and hence, with care prospects and steering, you will be easily able to construct an efficient business plan.

Therefore, these are some of the important strategies and tactics that can cater to the help of scheduling a business plan and with the passage of time, one can easily nourish the concept of business making in no time. One needs to understand the business making and its scheduling is not a piece of cake and it can be, at time, very complicated as well. However, if there is an iron will and gentle affiliation in the making, then no amount of hard work will go in vain.

Hints about Reading People

Human Behavior

Human behavior has interpreted a kind of behavior in which a human is perceived in a social, economic and logical context. The behavior starts to evolve from babyhood to adolescence and it has many impacts on it. The babyhood method is used to see the nature and nurture of the baby, through which he is able to attain a strong reservation in the prospects of life. The human behavior of youth is dependent on three modes. The first mode if of cultural progression. Under what culture, the human is able to grow and how the culture impacts the gender of the human is all that cultural progression is about. In this phase, the cultural ingredients that are the role of economics, religion, politics and society are carefully discussed. This cultural progression is able to garner most of the capabilities of the people and with the passage of time, the public is able to transform the ideas of human behavior effectively. Therefore, cultural progression is a valid argument, which gives brief institutions to work holistically.

The second mode is cognitive development in which the people are able to be interpreted in the construct of small and large cognition holistically. The cognition comes with respect to time and the person is interpreted according to cognition. This means that more the person thinks, the cognition process wants to be established effectively and with the passage of time, the people are able to have more insight into this respective issue. So, cognition development is a process through which a person's mind is actually construed and with the process of time and phase, he is understood to be a human.

The third mode is of gender development. By gender development, it is asserted the evolutionary phases, that the person is able to integrate into his or her character through the passage of time, is referred to be as gender development. Gender development is a strong process through which both men and women learn effectively. The men ratio is all about rage and individualistic opinion while the women want to be more progressive and expressive in their nature. Therefore, they tend to mold the constructs of their behavior and with the passage of time, the people are able to have more inclination to the coming time. Thus, the use of gender development is important to be understood in a pragmatic manner.

So, these are three modes of human development and these modes are able to be effective in the coming mode of time due to which they are able to have more generic comprehensions in their making. This concept is more aggressive in its demand and it can demand many overtures in its coming phase.

Theories of Human development

This portion of the chapter will deal strongly with the constructs of human development in which the person is able to have strong modes of comprehension with the public. These theories will be developed by eminent philosophers and scientists in the coming time. The individual that use these kinds of behavior were Sigmund Freud, Charles Darwin and many more. Their theories along with their comprehensions are as follows:

Sigmund believed that every person is born with a notion known as libido. This libido is tantamount to the emotional development of the child and the child is able to harness the emotional development of libido and thus, with the passage of time, he develops the aspirations of love and adoration. The aspiration is more systematic in their nature and the child learns the wrongs and rights of life. This libido makes the child more pragmatic in its nature and the child can delve into many aspirations in later life. The child learns the love matters with the mom of the family, he tends to be more affiliated with the opposite gender and there is a sense of authorization of the person with the family member. Therefore, the construction of libido is a concept, which is more effective for people to learn it holistically. The idea is simple in its regard and hence the people are able to make the inclinations in it with respect to time.

Freud also developed a structure of personality for the people. The people are able to have a strong mode of reservation with the other modes of society. Freud believed that every person has its own sense of longing with other personalities and the personalities change with respect to time. The time of personality development is able to induce people with more and more assertions with respective time. The time table of the person varies with strong conservations and the person is able to have more evolution in the coming time. Therefore, the personality assessment of the person is able to be achieved with respect to time. Freud believed that in order to have a strong goal in personality development, one needs to harbor subjectivity in its core relations. The subjectivity could come with respect to time and the person can learn through it. If the subjectivity is all minimum and the person is not able to have enough interactions with the people then there is no usage of a strong personality. The personality orders will deplete with respect of time and the person would not be able to make hard assertions in the coming time. Thus, the personality assessment needs to be checked while catering to the making of a personality and Freud believes that it is an important way to check the balances of the person in the coming time.

Erick Erikson was also of the belief of how people can be elevated in the construct of emotional belief. He believed that people are able to have sound knowledge on the topic of assertion and personality making. However, the situations in the coming time are quite different. Erik wanted the person to have an emotional check on them through which many people, will be able to have sound careers in the book. The idea is that the person is not able to make sound assertions in the coming time. He believed that the person must have an emotional character making in the time and this will help them to make the issues to make more interesting and capable in the coming time. Therefore, Erick will make you believe that the person will be able to induce more progression in the coming time.

Erik had eight stages of development for the human. These are: infancy, trust versus mistrust, early childhood, preschool and school age. He believed that the person is able to learn a lot through these days and with the passage of time, the person is able to have a strong check on his mind as well. These eight stages govern the body language as well as the human behavior of the individual in a coherent manner. The trust versus mistrust is a mindset and a process in which the child is able to learn the major advantages of socialization and ideas that who to trust and who not to. The trust factor comes with the process of time and it helps the individual to learn many ground realities of the time and human behavior. Therefore, it is important to understand how the public is able to be shamed by the narrative of human development.

Another scientist in this educational venture is Piaget, who belongs to Switzerland and he is able to make the mobilities of the personality a bad place. He wants to study the intellectual functioning and reasoning of the individual that how the person is able to have strong intellectual cognition with a person in an effective manner. The effect of the cognition is so sound and great that the person is able to carve out a personal space of livelihood to other personalities in the coming time. The cognition helps to have a systematic endeavor in the coming time and therefore, a person is able to have a strong impact on its personality with the coming time. Thus, cognition is a side to a person's ability with which he is able to make a strong inclination in the person's mind. Hence, it is important for you to understand that why the person is not able to have a strong grip on intellectual freedom and this is exactly a thesis that Mr. Piaget is able to develop with the passage of time.

Next comes the contextualization of learning theory. This is the theory that advocates the sum of all the construction of humans in the coming time. This theory asserts the possibility of strong cognition and mobility in the coming time and any person, who has a strong sense of living is able to have a concentrated pillar of extractions in the coming time. The learning theory is able to make sound credentials in the coming time. This theory helps individuals to make reasons for living and adopting free in the coming time. The people want to make the credence of the personalities more functioning in the coming time and according to them, the person is able to have a sense of pleasure if all its learning and progression are learned in an effective manner. The idea here is not that the person is not able to make strong contention in the coming time but he is sure of dealing with the person float in an effective manner. This sense of actualization comes in the person when he is learning and hence, learning theory helps to deal with the person more effectively and holistically.

So, these are some of the theories, spearheaded by political scientists that can lead to the comprehension of the public. Human development is a complex manner, which is able to be perceived collectively by humans and humans tend to resolve more contextualization for human development. These theories will help to resolve the function come in a generic way and the person will understand effectively the constructs of the individual in a standard manner. Therefore, human development is a process that is able to have a strong generalization of the instruments in a cool manner. The idea is simply that one needs to be well functioning and adaptable in its current outlook and in order to have more strong ingredients of human development, one also needs to form strong approaches to it. Thus, the next section of the book will deal with the incisive approaches which help us understand the mode of human development easily.

Approaches to Understand Human Behavior

There are five major approaches to understand human behavior.

3. The Psychodynamic Approach

The psychodynamic approach was propounded by Sigmund Freud in which he believed that there are three personalities that develop the approach of the person. One is the development of the illness factor. This factor was discovered in the year 1993, when Freud was able to discuss the advantages of the illness emanating of the child. This theory was further comprehended with the passage of time and the people believed that it was able to make the functionalities of the personality look better. Another theory was about the conscious and the subconscious manner. This theory believed that people are able to delve into the personalities of the person in an effective manner. The conscious mind is the mind that is aware of all the pros and cons of living. Whereas, the subconscious mind is the mind, which heralds some of the important aspirations of daily life. According to Freud, the subconscious mind clearly stores a lot of information in the minds of the public and with the passage of time, the person is able to have a strong version of interest in it. The idea of the construction is quite similar to the game because the psychodynamic approach will give you strong comprehension about the functioning of the mind. The system will thereby make you believe in it and with the passage of time, you will be able to have a stronghold on the construction effectively. Therefore, the psychodynamic approach helps you to psychologically listen to the minds of the people and understand them effectively.

4. Behavioral Approach

This is a kind of approach which makes the behaviors of other people understandable through experiences and external stimulus. By many psychologists it is also referred to as the classical conditioning method and the conditioning is done by altering the external stimulus of the public. The public gets to know the major ingredients of the development of behaviorism and with the passage of time, the people get to know the true nature of all the components of real life. The idea is simple and straight here that to make sure that how the people are able to have more strategic interest in their coming, the behavioral approach is possibly maintained and implemented. Therefore, the behavioral approach is an approach, which needs to be strengthened by all means and it tends to give strong reservations in the coming time. So, the reason for making the humans look more understandable and adjustable, the people must not make the hectic decision of life and try its best in making the reasons go way bound.

Predicting Human Behavior

The human behavior of humans can be predicted in the following ways.

The use of Homecourt

This is the manipulation technique in which the individual uses his or her home as an advantage for his own benefits. The psychological demeanor was used to define the crux of the people, who were under the liability of the people. For the substantiation of this case, it is important to understand that the people, who are in a psychological condition to manipulate others are very smart. The first rule is that the public must come into consideration of the psychological master and then the master will navigate his thoughts. First and foremost, the master uses the court to manipulate the personalities and then the public first advocates the use of manipulation to be just and obscure.

Establishing the stance first and then looking for weaknesses

In the manipulation of psychology, it is important to understand that the establishment of the stance is first. The stance needs to be manifested first and then it is established so that the people, who are listening to the track come under the way of the manipulator. Once the stance of the manipulator is established then the maneuvering is very easy. The people have to understand the use of the stance easily and then they have to use the words of the manipulator as a source of manipulation. The people can easily be thrown into the abyss when the manipulator asks a lot of questions. The idea is that the public first navigates the stance and then the manipulator can use the stance to find its justification. If the manipulator wants to find the essence of the stance and if he finds some distortion of the stance then he can avoid the crux of the stance very badly.

Manipulation of Facts

If you want to assert the significance of the psychology of manipulation, then the facts stated can be used to deceive. The facts can be of any statement and that can be used to defy the logic of the people. For instance, if the manipulator is using the fact sound of one thing then that thing can be used to defy as well. People that can assess the logic of the personalities can manipulate by navigating them through their own lies. This is the act of manipulation if people are using the effects of deviance in an effective manner.

Overwhelming with facts and statistics

First and foremost, the fact and statistics can be used to defy the personalities of the public. The facts are to be constructed in an effective manner so that the manipulator can be used to defy the odds of manipulation. So, for a strong manipulation, you have to overwhelm the facts and statistics with the people. The people can be used to come under the clout of statistics if the public is not able to use a strong mode of psychological messages. Therefore, it is important that psychology can be used to interpret the essence of the public in a logical manner.

Overwhelming with procedures and Red tape

In order to maintain the crux of other personalities, the manipulator uses procedures and red tapes to give more defying reasons to the public. The manipulator will use the procedural versions, in which the public has to be manipulated in a stringent manner. The manipulator can be harnessed in a strong way so that the public can give concrete methods to it. For this reason, to be constructed, the manipulator uses some procedures and advantages through which the normal public comes into oppression. This oppression is used to defy the lands of the public and the public comes under the manipulation of the manipulator. So, in order to manipulate the people, the psychologists can use the crux of procedures and some secretive tapes that can be used in a strong manner.

Raising the voice and Displaying Negative Emotions

The manipulator in order to make the voice of the public effective has to raise the voice of himself. The manipulator uses some strong means and modes through which he is able to forecast a shadow of darkness. This darkness is used to construct the methods of manipulation among the stakeholders and the people can come under effective modes of destruction. Also, the negative emotions, give the value of harsh realities among the public and they get severely neglected by the personalities. Therefore, it is important to understand that the public is not able to get manipulated if they see the raised level of voice and hence there is a display of festering emotions among the people.

Negative Surprises

The negative surprises are another mode of manipulation by the manipulator. The manipulate can be using harsh negative surprises through which the people are not able to understand their nature. These negative surprises also affect the effects of the mentality of the public and with the passage of time, the people do not get easily comfortable in this essence. The negative surprises show a strong moment of disinterest among the public and there is a culture of disassociation among the public through the negative surprises. The negative surprises give a sense of bad omens for the public through which the people are not able to give standard modes of deviation for the public.

Giving you a little or no time to decide

The time that has been given to you is either less time or there is no time. The manipulator wants to get his thing done because only then he is effective in his mode. The manipulator would cast his own means to come in front of the public. The time that has been slotted for the manipulator has a strong version of connectedness with the people and thus, there needs to be a strong sense of affection for the people. Therefore, the time of decision that has been given to you is a tool of the manipulator so that the public is able to give more directions for the public. So, the time has to be a motive interest for the public to understand in an effective manner.

Use of Negative Humor

The negative humor is a manipulating tool to disassociate you from your being. The manipulator would cast negative humor on you and will do his best to make you feel bad about the situation. This manipulation is further designed by the manipulator to disempower you and with its continuous bolstering, the use of negative humor could be very harsh and brutal for you. Therefore, the use of negative humor could be used to induce isolationism and fanaticism in public and could be very pernicious for you as well. If the use of negative humor could be bad for you then manipulation could be a stringent maneuver to showcase in-effectiveness among you.

Consistent Judgement

The consistent judgment could be a harsh tactic to induce fright among you. The manipulator could use the essence of judgement to make you feel discomfort able. How it can be done? This is as follows: Suppose, you are sitting in a room and the manipulator is sitting in front of you and you are able to hear the statements of the manipulator and with the passage of time, the public is not able to define the essence of the judgments properly. The public is quite effective in harboring the essence of the manipulator and if the manipulator is successful is dissing you with his judgments then finally you are under his claw. The consistent judgment will make you feel very demotivated and with the passage of time, you will be feeling delusional.

Silent Treatments

When the manipulator wants to harbor his mechanism then he uses the edifice of silence. This silence is very haunting. It is very managerial and with the passage of time, it induces a bad version of manipulation among you. You get affected by the silence of the manipulator and in time, this becomes very pestering among you. The silent treatment is also very haunting at an individualistic level because at times, the public is not able to see the results of it in a discomforting manner. Therefore, silent treatments can be used to haunt the premises of the individual in a bad manner.

Thus, these are some of the mechanisms that make the prediction of human behavior look way too easy. Therefore, human development needs to be adopted with the passage of time properly.

Conclusion

To conclude the book, influencing can be termed both positive and negative for a person. The influencing can be done for a student, teacher and politician. The weapons of influence are very haunting their apparatus but they can be very positive as well. The use of ethical influence along with use of positive inclinations can be used to up bring the model of human nature with the people and with the passage of time, the person can learn a lot form them. The business personalities, who have given a lot to influencing people must be learnt properly and their admirations must be discovered properly.